PSYCHOSOCIA
IDENTITY DIFFUSION IN ADOLESCENTS

Tarika Sharma

CONTENTS

CHAPTER 1

INTRODUCTION

INTRODUCTION

Adolescence is a multifaceted phase for which there are numerous definitions. The term *adolescence* originated from the Latin word "adolescere", which means to grow or to mature (Paludi, 2002). It is defined as a transitional life phase of human development that usually happens during the period from puberty to maturity in adulthood (Erikson, 1968). Various researchers focus on different perspectives in defining adolescence, making it very difficult to have one absolute definition. Macleod (2003) explains that adolescents are neither children nor adults and that the developmental phase of adolescence serves as a bridge between the two stages. Originally, it was not regarded as a distinct developmental period because, already at a young age, children were forced into adult roles, such as marriage (Louw & Louw, 2007). During the industrialization period, children's rights became more important, and adolescence emerged as a developmental phase (Richter, 2006; Sigelman & Rider, 2009).

Some authors suggest that adolescence can be explained by using chronological age (Sadock & Sadock, 2007). Adolescence is divided into three stages, namely early, middle, and late adolescence. Early adolescence is regarded as the period between 12 and 14 years of age and is characterized by the most prominent initial physical and behavioral changes (Sadock & Sadock, 2007). Early adolescence is also typified as a period of overwhelming confusion and rejection of the family (Sadock & Sadock, 2007). Middle adolescence is indicated as the time between 14 and 16 years of age. During middle adolescence, adolescents are preoccupied mostly with becoming autonomous (WHO, 2014b). Finally, late adolescence occurs between 17 and 19 years of age and is associated mostly with exploration in various domains to develop a stable sense of self (Sadock & Sadock, 2007). However, authors like Newman and Newman (2012) argue that adolescence could be divided into two separate categories, namely early adolescence (12 to 18 years of age) and later adolescence (18 to 24 years of age). For Newman and Newman (2012), early adolescence commences with the start of puberty in both genders and ends when individuals finish high school. The psychosocial crisis associated with the early adolescence stage is group identity versus alienation. This psychosocial crisis relates to the desire of individuals to have meaningful relationships but also develop a unique sense of self (Newman & Newman, 2012). Later adolescence begins when individuals leave high school at about 18 years of age and ends at 24 years of age. The later adolescence stage is characterized by adolescents becoming independent from their parents and establishing a stable personal ego identity (Newman & Newman, 2012).

The scientific study of adolescence was pioneered by G. Stanley Hall (1904) who viewed these formative years as the best decade of life during which the functions of every sense undergo reconstruction brought on by physiological factors. As their bodies, minds, and societal roles are changing and developing, adolescents are expected to figure out who they are and what they want from life. In essence, they start forming their *identity*. A well-developed identity gives on a sense of one's strengths and individual's uniqueness. This formation of personal goals, values, and beliefs is influenced by the various contexts in which adolescents develop, such as within families, schools, and peer groups. Although the amount of time spent at home generally decreases as teenagers approach and enter late adolescence, parents still remain highly influential in guiding their children to successfully traverse the biological, cognitive, and social transitions that are co-occurring with the *identity formation process* (Hill, 1983).

THE CONCEPT OF IDENTITY

Identity concerns are a fundamental dimension and psychosocial task for an adolescent's life. Beginning in their early teens, adolescents start to ask questions such as ''Who am I?'' ''What am I doing in my life?'' ''What kind of relationships do I want?'' ''What kind of work do I want to do?'' and ''what are my beliefs?''(Archer, 1982). It is a complex construct and has been defined by various authors. Erikson (1968) refers to identity as "ego synthesis" and argues that identity is the dynamic interaction between ego identity synthesis and ego identity confusion. Thus, it signifies a stable sense of self over time and across situations. It is also described as an overall sense of who you are, currently and in the future, as well as how individuals fit into their social environment (Erikson, 1968). Thus, identity is the accomplishment of being comfortable with your current, present, and future self (King, 2006).

Marcia (2002) refers to ego identity as a sense of who one is, based on the past, and who one realistically can be in the future. Thus it is a combination of the adolescents' history, beliefs, and values in a self-configuration. It is conceptualized further as the consideration of alternatives of who one might become and a process of making decisions about who one is (Luyckx, Goossens, Soenens, Beyers & Vansteenkiste, 2005). Therefore, it is a conscious sense of the individual's uniqueness (Crocetti, Sica et al., 2012). It is also explained as a self-organized construct, an assimilated psychological structure of personal values and goals that occur through social interaction (Kaplan & Flum, 2010). Furthermore, Koepke and Denissen (2012) indicate that ego identity is the self-structure that combines experience into cognitive schemas. For example, cognitive schemas help individuals to filter information and make personal meaning of new information to form their own unique ego identities.

Identity is not only a self-structure, but also a social construct. Munday (2006) argues that it is both a personal and social construct, which makes individuals unique and similar to one another. It is a process during which individuals define themselves in relation to others in their specific social environments (Munday, 2006). Josselson (2012) argues that identity is the interaction between individuals' sense of self and their social environment. Therefore, identity can be explained as a conciliation process of self-definition within the limits of individuals' social contexts (Jenkins, 2008).

DIMENSIONS OF IDENTITY

The term *identity* has many separate dimensions that make up adolescents' total sense of self and contribute towards the broad understanding of identity (Paludi, 2002). Thus, it can be classified into three overall interdependent dimensions, namely personal, social, and relational identity.

   PERSONAL IDENTITY: It entails intrapersonal devotions made by individuals to develop their own unique sense of self (Erikson, 1968; Marcia, 1966).

   SOCIAL IDENTITY: It can be defined as membership to a specific social group, where identity development is influenced by the group's expectations (Tajfel & Tuner, 1979).

RELATIONAL IDENTITY: It is conceptualized as the personal connotation allocated to various roles individuals fulfill each day (Chen, Boucher & Tapias, 2006). All three of the identity dimensions (personal, social, and relational) are interrelated and influence processes involved in developing individuals' ego identity. Individuals' personal identities develop within their social contexts, which offer the opportunity for developing social and relational identities.

CHARACTERISTICS OF IDENTITY:

1) Identity is a social-psychological construct that reflects social influences through imitation and identification processes and active self-construction in the creation of what is important to the self and to others.

2) The active self-constructive aspects of identity is founded upon cognitive or ego operations that organize, structure, and construct/reconstruct knowledge of the self.

3) Identity, as a psychological structure, is a self-regulatory system which functions to direct attention, filter or process information, manage impressions, and select appropriate behaviors.

4) An individual's personal or social identity not only is shaped, in part, by the living systems around the individual, but the individual's identity can shape and change the nature of these living systems.

5) Differentiation and integration serve to shape the identity of life systems. Thus, identity is a necessary part of human social groups in that it contributes to the structural characteristics of permeability, continuity, and coherence of each life system. Permeability is the adaptive nature of the system in its relationship to

other systems. Continuity and coherence give the structure identifiable features over time.

6) Like all social psychological constructs, identity has its own functional purpose. The five most common functions of identity include:

   (a) providing the structure for understanding who one is;

   (b) providing meaning and direction through commitments, values and goals;

   (c) providing a sense of personal control and free will;

   (d) striving for consistency, coherence, and harmony between values, beliefs, and commitments;

   (e) enabling the recognition of potential through a sense of future, possibilities, and alternative choices.

BRIEF HISTORY OF IDENTITY

Eric Erikson was a brilliant psychoanalyst, and is still perennially cited as the *Architect of Identity development theory*. He became one of the earliest psychologists to take an explicit interest in identity. Erikson set forth a theory of ego development to account for the interactions between psychological, social, historical and developmental factors in the formation of personality. Perhaps no single theoretician has had a greater impact on our perceptions of adolescent personality development than him. In particular, Erikson's (1968) **Identity: Youth and Crisis** has provided a theoretical framework for theorizing about, and for measuring identity formation.

Originally, Erikson was stimulated by the difficulties which some World War II veterans encountered upon reentering society, and became interested in problems associated with acute identity diffusion. Over time and through clinical experience he came to believe that the pathological difficulties which some veterans had in leaving one role (soldier) and entering another (civilian) were psychologically similar to the problem which some adolescents experience as they leave childhood and move through the transition of adolescence into adulthood. From this experiential framework has evolved a psychology of adolescent identity formation. Drawing on his psychoanalytic thinking with an emphasis on ego development, he derived several definitions of identity.

"What I have called ego identity, however, concerns more than the mere fact of existence. Ego identity then, in its subjective aspect, is the awareness of the fact that there is a selfsameness and continuity to the ego's synthesizing methods, the style of one's individuality, and that this style coincides with the sameness and continuity of one's meaning for significant others in the immediate community."

Erik Erikson (1968, p. 50; emphasis in original)

Crisis is defined as a normative life event designating: "a necessary turning point, a crucial moment, when development must move one way or another, marshaling resources of growth, recovery, and further differentiation." (Erikson, 1968). This normative identity crisis is thought to stimulate identity consciousness that compels the individual to explore life alternatives (e.g., political views, religious choices, etc.) and is resolved through personal ideological commitment.

Erikson's theory of psychosocial development uniquely addresses adolescence as a specific developmental phase within a life stage framework. His theory is based on eight stages spanning from birth to old age identified eight major crises that build upon each other during the lifespan, such that the outcomes of all childhood stages contribute to the establishment of an identity during adolescence. His depiction of the life cycle resembles a mythical quest in which individuals face eight never-ending challenges or crises. These crises are turning points which force one to recognize and choose between two opposing alternatives. Resolving a crisis involves combining elements of the positive alternative with parts of the negative alternative. When the positive pole dominates, resolution is considered favorable, but when the negative poledominates resolution is unfavorable.

Identity Cohesion vs. Identity Diffusion marks the fifth in Erikson's eight-stage lifespan sequence of developmental tasks, which comes to the fore during adolescence. During this time, adolescents will seek to find some resolution between these two poles. Optimally, adolescents undergo the *identity-formation process.* This process involves the ego's ability to synthesize and integrate important earlier identifications into a new form, uniquely one's own. The crisis of identity vs. identity confusion, one of these developmental struggles, ascends during the life stage of adolescence. Individuals gain certain strengths when they resolve psychosocial crises favorably (Erikson, 1968). Identity fluctuates during the teenage years as adolescents actively explore alternatives by trying out various roles offered by their society. Identity fluctuates during the teenage years as adolescents actively explore alternatives by trying out various roles offered by their society. In their search for continuity and sameness, the adolescent attempts to incorporate the morality learned in childhood with personal aptitudes and the opportunities offered in social roles (Erikson, 1963).

Although Erikson's (1968) approach to identity development is a useful description of development during the human life cycle, it is criticized for not being a measurable research construct (Kaplan & Flum, 2010; Schwartz, 2002). To facilitate understanding of the construct *ego identity*, other researchers such as Marcia (1966) and Berzonsky (1989) have expanded on Erikson's psychosocial theory.

THEORETICAL FRAMEWORK/MODELS ON IDENTITY

Over the years since Erikson first presented the concept of identity, there have been many attempts to operationalize and empirically examine each of them. Attempts to study Erikson's fifth psychosocial task of Identity vs. Role Confusion have been undertaken in different ways. One line of research has examined the place that "Identity vs. Role Confusion" holds in the eight-stage lifespan scheme (Constantinople, 1967,; Rosenthal, Gurney, &C Moore, 1981). A second line of work has focused on Erikson's fifth psychosocial stage alone and has conceptualized it in bipolar terms - as something one "has" to a greater or lesser degree (e.g., Simmons, 1970). A third, very general approach has attempted to study one or more dimensions of ego identity outlined by Erikson (e.g., Blasi & Milton, 1991). Within this third tradition, a very popular approach has emerged in the attempt to understand the relationship between exploration and commitment variables to the formation of ego identity. The identity-status model developed by Marcia (1966, 1967) identifies four different styles (or statuses) by which late adolescents approach identity-defining roles and values.

Marcia: Identity Status Paradigm

Marcia's (1966) theory of identity status has become one of the most successful and widely used approaches of studying the formation of ego identity in adolescents (Crocetti, Scrignaro et al., 2012). The advantage of using Marcia's (1966) model is that it provides for a larger selection of styles in dealing with identity issues than Erikson's bipolar model of identity vs. identity confusion. Marcia's (1966) model is well established, has been used over a period of 45 years and inspired approximately 1000 theoretical and empirical studies (Arseth et al., 2009; Berzonsky & Adams, 1999; Kroger & Marcia, 2011; Marcia, 1993a, 1993b, 1980). Therefore, it could be argued that Marcia's (1966) model of ego identity status is well researched, supported by numerous studies, has established characteristics for each ego identity status, and is related to various other models of development of ego identity (Crocetti, Sica et al., 2012; Kaplan & Flum, 2010; Kroger & Marcia, 2011; Luyckx et al., 2005; Marcia, 2002).

He suggests that an ego identity is a combination of an adolescent's history, beliefs, and values in a self-structure. Adolescents with well-developed self-structures/ identities are more aware of their own uniqueness, similarities, strengths, and weaknesses and use these qualities adaptively in fulfilling their social roles (Kaplan & Flum, 2010; Marcia, 1980). Adolescents with less developed self-structures/identities, lack self-evaluation, are more confused about their own abilities, and rely on external sources to evaluate themselves (Marcia, 1980). Ego identity permits adolescents to infer information they collect and directs them in responding suitably (Shanahan & Pychyl, 2007).

Aspects of Marcia's theory:

Marcia's (1966) theory of ego identity status could be explained by three overarching aspects.

First, ego identity consists of different identity domains, namely the ideological and interpersonal domain.

Second, adolescents move on a continuum between two dimensions, namely exploration and commitment. Exploration refers to the action of gathering information, and commitment is the integration of personal values, beliefs, and goals in various life domains (Marcia, 1966).

Finally, Marcia (1966) identifies four ego identity statuses (foreclosed, diffused, moratorium, and achieved) based on the inclusion or exclusion of the two dimensions of exploration and commitment.

IDENTITY DOMAINS

Marcia's (1966) model of identity status assesses identity across a number of life domains. These life domains are the most significant areas of development of ego identity in which adolescents practice their ego identity options (Low, Akande, & Hill, 2005). Marcia's (1966) original theory explains identity in the context of the ideological domain, which consists of vocational, religious, and political aspects. Grotevant and Adams (1984) argue that identity development also includes interpersonal aspects, and they classify identity into two main domains, namely the ideological and interpersonal domains. They suggest that ideological identities include individuals' values and belief systems in terms of religious, political, and vocational aspects, and explain interpersonal identities as all relationships, for example romantic relationships, friendships, gender roles, and recreational options. Thus, the forming identity process operates within the various life domains of an adolescent's specific social environment (Schwartz et al., 2013).

DIMENSIONS OF MARCIA'S EGO IDENTITY MODEL

Erikson (1968) and Marcia (1966) suggest that forming an identity is an active process, illustrated by continuous changes in the amount of exploration and commitment, during which important choices need to be made. Exploration and commitment are fundamental to Marcia's model of identity development (Marcia, 1966). Thus, identity is formed by a process of exploring alternatives and making commitments (Marcia, 2002).

> **Exploration** – It entails the active exploration of possible identity options in different identity domains. It also refers to the investigation and reflection of important choices and meaningful alternatives with the intention of making firm commitments (Crocetti, Jahromi, & Meeus, 2012; Kaplan & Flum, 2010). Laghi et al. (2013) suggest that exploration could be viewed as problem-solving behaviour concerning various identity domains to form a more coherent sense of self. It is also suggested that exploration is a process of discovering a representation of what the individual's unique sense of self might be in the future (Berman, Schwartz, Kurtines, & Berman, 2001). Adolescents use the environment (family, parents, and peers) to attain information to assist them with their decision-making process. Decision making is achieved by adolescents' vigorous questioning in various life domains to consider alternatives before making a final commitment (Arseth et al., 2009; Crocetti, Scrignaro et al., 2012; Crocetti, Sica et al., 2012). Exploration is

defined further as the intentional external and internal act of collecting and processing information in relation to an individual's unique sense of self to construct meaning, which promotes development of ego identity (Kaplan & Flum, 2010). Therefore, exploration can be explained as the process of considering various alternatives and social environments to achieve a stable sense of self.

Commitment- It is a personal investment in an ego identity and participation in important actions aimed at executing the commitment. Marcia (1980) also argues that making a commitment to an ego identity provides someone with a sense of direction and purpose in life. Thus, commitment to a personal ego identity will assist an adolescent to handle issues that arise in the implementation of his or her ego identity. According to Schwartz (2001), commitment can be described as a long-term life choice in terms of adolescents' goals and value systems. Commitment can be explained further as a decision to pursue a meaningful future (Laghi et al., 2013).

Marcia (1966) thus explains how formation of ego identity is resolved, supported by the absence or presence of personal exploration and commitment to a unique ego identity and personal belief system (Crocetti, Sica et al., 2012; Lubenko & Sebre, 2007). Luyckx, Schwartz, Goossens and Pollock (2008) argue that exploration is associated with ego identity confusion and symptoms of anxiety and depression during adolescence. However, commitment is related to life satisfaction and stability. Therefore, adolescents' exploration and commitment to various decisions have repercussions with regard to forming ego identity (Marcia, 1980).

MARCIA IDENTITY STATUS

Following are four identity statuses are based on adolescents' exploration and commitment to their decisions in the various life domains of ego identity (Marcia, 1980). The four ego identity statuses signify different manners of dealing with the identity crisis described by Erikson (Marcia, 1966)

Identity Achievement

Identity Foreclosure

Identity Moratorium

Identity Diffusion

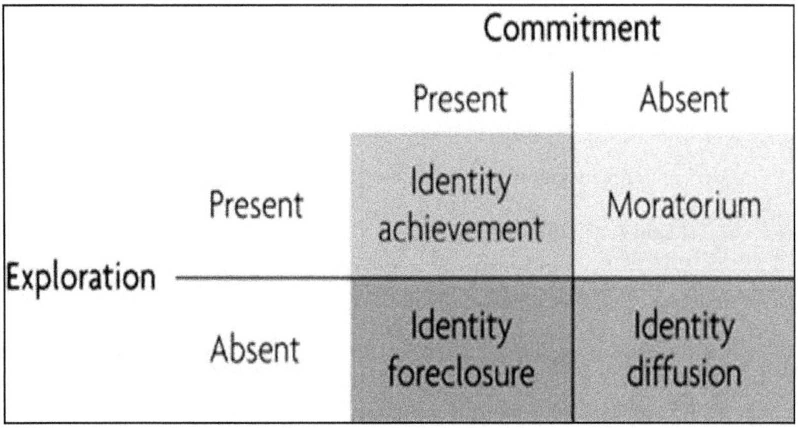

		Commitment	
		Present	Absent
Exploration	Present	Identity achievement	Moratorium
	Absent	Identity foreclosure	Identity diffusion

Fig 1.1 Marcia's Identity Status Paradigm

Identity Achievement– Individuals with an achieved status have experienced an exploration period, and continue making strong ideological commitments (Maria, 1966). Individuals with an achieved status are described as having experienced an exploration period (crisis) and are pursuing self-chosen ideological goals (Marcia, 1980). Furthermore, they are characterized by firm commitments to life choices after a period of exploration (Crocetti, Jahromi et al., 2012; Marcia, 1966). It is the most developmentally mature and adaptive ego identity status of the four ego identity statuses. Individuals in the achieved status portray internal locus of control, rational decision-making, realistic thinking (Blustein & Phillips, 1990; Laghi et al., 2013), and good moral reasoning (Kroger, 2007). They show a high sense of conscientiousness and openness, and these individuals have a positive attitude towards adjustment (Kroger & Marcia, 2011; Luyckx et al., 2005; Wan Yunus et al., 2010). They are also characterized by having mature relationships and balanced thinking (Krettenauer, 2005).

Crocetti, Jahromi et al. (2012) suggest that individuals with an achieved status relate to pro-social behavior and social responsibility. They are characterized by well-being, high self-esteem and motivation, as well as less idealistic views of their parents (Campbell, Adams, & Dobson, 1984; Kroger and Marcia, 2011; Laghi et al.2013).

Identity Foreclosure– The foreclosed status can be defined as individuals making strong commitments to introjected personal values in the absence of an exploration period (Marcia, 1966). The foreclosed status is described as adolescents who, without questioning, are committed to ideological goals (Marcia, 2002). These adolescents are set to commitments with little or no exploration (Crocetti, Jahromi et al., 2012). Marcia (2002) suggests that adolescents prefer the same social environment during as in childhood and adopt authoritarian values. These individuals' life choices are usually influenced by introjections from respected figures like their parents or role models, rather than self-chosen (Marcia, 1980; Wan Yunus, Malik, & Zakaria, 2013). They do not explore different options to form their own unique ego identities (Wan Yunus et al., 2013). Still, Marcia

(2002) and Kroger and Marcia (2011) argue that foreclosed can be viewed as committed individuals characterized by positive well-being and a stable ego identity. Schwartz et al. (2011) suggest that they experience self-satisfaction and low levels of internalized symptoms.

Adolescents with a foreclosed status are the least anxious, because of the absence of exploration (Bergh & Erling, 2005). However, they can be defensive; they are rigid in their thinking and may have low levels of openness, high levels of conformity and external locus of control (Kaplan & Flum, 2010; Luyckx et al., 2005; Laghi et al. 2013). They are dependent on their parents and these adolescents are prone to lack confidence. Although they have a positive relationship with their parents, the relationship is based on dependence and idealization rather than mutuality (Frank, Pirsch, & Wright, 1990; Berzonsky & Adams 1999).

Identity Moratorium– The moratorium status is a state of active exploration with little commitments to an ego identity (Marcia, 1966). Individuals with a moratorium ego identity status experience an identity crisis, but have not yet made any commitments in their ideological domain (Marcia, 1980). They participate in high degrees of exploration with no commitments to any decisions in terms of their life choices (Crocetti, Jahromi et al., 2012). It could be argued that adolescents with a moratorium ego status experience emotional turmoil because of experiencing insecurities about not having firm commitment to live choices (Meeus, Iedema, Maassen, & Engels, 2005). Adolescents' inability to commit to a stable ego identity is often associated with high levels of anxiety (Laghi et al., 2013; Marcia, 1966; Wan Yunus et al., 2013). Luyckx et al. (2005) suggest that individuals with a moratorium ego identity status are associated with symptoms of depression and low self-esteem. In addition, family relationships of adolescents with a moratorium ego status are often characterized by ambivalence (Marcia, 1994).

However, individuals with a moratorium status are associated not only with negative psychological outcomes, but also with openness and curiosity during adolescence (Luyckx, Goossens, & Soenens, 2006a). Kaplan and Flum (2010) also argue that individuals portray the moratorium ego status show autonomy and positive problem solving skills. This identity status represents high degree of exploration but a low degree of commitment. Adolescents have acquired vague or ill-formed ideological and occupational commitments; they are still undergoing the identity search (crisis). They are beginning to commit to an identity but are still developing it. Moratoriums are struggling to define themselves. They are lively, engaging, conflicted, and sometimes tiring to be around. They may try to draw others into their identity formation project, sometimes setting others up to take a position polar to their own stated one, so that they may be at least temporarily relieved of the internal conflict they are undergoing by converting an interior struggle into an external one. They are often exquisitely morally sensitive. And, if they are articulate, they can engage others in their quest and appear, albeit briefly, as charismatic figures. There are other moratoriums that appear to be drowning in their struggles to swim against the tide of earlier authority based identifications. Rather than explorers, they become ruminators, perpetually mired in what seem to be insoluble dilemmas. In the best of outcomes, they make self-relevant choices and move on to the firm commitments of identity achievement; in more unfortunate outcomes, they can become paralyzed in their vacillations.

Identity Diffusion– Individuals in the diffused status have not experienced an exploration period or made personal commitments (Marcia, 1966). Individuals portraying the diffused status are characterized by no commitments to any ideological goals, regardless of whether they have experienced an exploration period (Marcia, 1980). They are reluctant or incapable to make commitments and do not explore vigorously to establish their ego identity (Marcia, 2002). Marcia (1966) describes these individuals as having the least developmentally mature and adaptive ego status of the four ego identity statuses. It is also argued that individuals with a diffused identity are described as dealing with their problems by avoidance (Marcia, 2002). They lack a stable ego identity and a secure sense of self. Individuals that portray a diffused status are associated with low self-esteem during adolescence (Kaplan & Flum, 2010; Laghi et al., 2013; Phillips & Pittman, 2007). Other authors also indicate that these individuals are associated with identity distress, hopelessness, antisocial attitudes, and behavioral problems (Kroger & Marcia, 2011; Phillips & Pittman, 2007).

Marcia called these identity "statuses" for a reason: the statuses are glimpses of the changing structure of self that can evolve over time (Marcia, 1980). An individual can have explored and committed to an identity (identity achievement) and then have a crisis (i.e. death of significant other, loss of a job, recently receiving very negative social feedback) that leads the individual into an identity crisis and a lost identity (identity moratorium). Therefore, the identity status is a snapshot in time of the individual's current sense of identity.

THEORIES BASED ON MARCIA'S IDENTITY STATUS PARADIGM

Researchers have elaborated on Marcia's ego identity status model to provide different perspectives on development of ego identity. However, Marcia's (1966) model is well established and still remains a reliable conceptualization of the development of ego identity as a construct.

Loevinger: Ego Development Model

Loevinger (1976) is another author who elaborates on Marcia's (1966) theory of ego identity status. He argued that development of ego identity is a subjective frame of reference through which individuals make sense of various experiences. Development of ego identity includes various domains of the development of personality, for example moral, cognitive, and emotional development and suggested that development of ego identity happens in hierarchical stages. Based on empirical studies, Loevinger (1976) identifies three levels of development of ego identity, namely the pre-conformist, conformist, and post-conformist levels. Each one of the levels consists of various stages that individuals have to pass hierarchically to master a stable ego identity successfully.

Pre-conformist level: At this level individuals can be in the impulsive or self-protective stage. In the impulsive stage, individuals are controlled by impulses and instantaneous experiences. Thereafter, individual's progresses to the self-protective stage, where they attain control over their impulses and learn that behavior have consequences.

Conformist level: Individuals at this level have to move through the conformist and self-awareness stages. During the conformist stage, individuals identify with the social norms of the group and do not self-differentiate. In the self-awareness stage, individuals start to recognize their uniqueness from the social group.

Post-conformist level: Individuals at this level have to master four stages to develop their ego identity successfully, namely the conscientious, individualistic, autonomous, and integrated stages. During the conscientious stage, individuals internalize certain values and goals that enable them to understand various perspectives and evaluate their own values. The following stage is called the individualistic stage, during which individuality and independence are the main features. The next stage is the autonomous stage, in which individuals show respect and greater tolerance for other people's ideas; therefore, reciprocity in their relationships becomes more important. The final stage is called the integrated stage, during which individuals have integrated their own unique ego identity.

Josselson: Theory of Women Identity Development

Josselson (1987), another researcher who theorizes ego identity, provides the foundation for understanding women's development of ego identity. Josselson (1987) elaborates on Marcia's (1966) ego identity status model to conceptualize formation of ego identity in women. Josselson (1987) identifies four ego identity pathways in women, namely drifters (diffusion), guardians (foreclosure), searchers (moratorium), and path makers (achievement). These ego identity pathways are based on the presence or exclusion of exploration and commitment (Josselson, 1987; Marcia, 1966).

Drifters: Women in this category have difficulty handling a crisis and making commitments. This category also called *lost and sometimes found.* They are severely dependent on others in supporting them to form a stable ego identity.

Guardians: Women in this category are have made commitments, but have never experienced an exploration period. They are influenced by parental beliefs and goals, which guide and direct their lives. This category is called *purveyors of the heritage*.

Searchers: They are also known as *daughters of the crisis*. They are aware of the choices and experience an exploration period, but internalize their family's standpoint and have trouble forming a unique sense of self.

Path makers: Women in this category gain autonomy from their parents and childhood introjections to form a unique sense of self. They are also known as *pavers of the way*.

Thus, Josselson's (1987) theory provides a unique way of understanding development of the ego identities of women, using Marcia's (1966) ego identity status model.

Berzonsky: Identity Style Model

Similar to Marcia's extrapolation of Erikson's work, Berzonsky extended Marcia's statuses with his Identity Style model (1989). Identity styles refer to social cognitive strategies an individual uses to explore and make decisions about information that is relevant to his or her sense of self. While Marcia's statuses are utilized as specific outcomes rather than processes, Berzonsky conceptualized three processing styles which reflect an individual's approach to problem-solving and decision-making.

Information oriented processing style

Normative oriented processing style

Avoidant/Diffuse oriented processing style

Information Oriented Processing Style– It is related to positive and successful coping strategies, problem-focused coping, and to openness to experience. It is negatively related to other-directedness, frailty effects of anxiety, dependence on wishful thinking, and emotional distancing. Adolescents utilizing an informational orientation are self-reflective and actively seek out and evaluate self-relevant information. Individuals with an information-orientated identity style use information to commit to their own unique goals and values in forming ego identities.

Normative Oriented Processing Style - It is related to highlight the expectations and standards of significant others. Those with a normative orientation more automatically adopt prescriptions and values from significant others and conform to these others' expectations. They have a low tolerance for ambiguity and a strong need for structure.

Diffuse Oriented Processing Style - It is related negatively to quality of peer relationships, academic achievement, and self-esteem. It positively related to maladaptive decisional strategies, drugs and alcohol problems, and depressive reactions. They procrastinate and delay dealing with identity issues for as long as possible. These individuals avoid exploration of any identity conflicts and do not actively shape their ego identities by anything but what their social environments require (Berman et al., 2001; Crocetti, Sica et al., 2012).

Berzonsky's styles overlap Marcia's statuses (Berzonsky, 1989).Specifically, achievers and moratoriums are seen as utilizing an *information orientation* style since they are utilizing or have utilized exploration as part of their identity building process. Informational style involves information seeking and problem-focused coping (Berzonsky, 1992). Individuals classified as using the informational orientation style would "actively seek out, process, and evaluate relevant information before making decisions." *Normative orientation* style relates to those in Marcia's fore closed status. Mirroring Marcia's description of foreclosures, individuals who have incorporated an identity created for them by others, normative orientation style describes individuals who have not actively explored facets of their identity, are very comfortable with their prescribed identity, and are fairly resistant to alternative aspects of identity. Lastly, *diffuse orientation* style describes the uncommitted passive (versus active) individuals in Marcia's diffusion category. Behaviors that reflect adopters of this style are characterized by a tendency to "delay and procrastinate until situational consequences and rewards dictate a course of action." (Berzonsky, 1989).

Abundant research documented the validity of distinguishing among these three identity styles. It has been shown that each style is characterized by a specific pattern of psychosocial and social cognitive correlates and consequences (Soenens, Duriez, & Goossens, 2005). However, little research devoted attention to potential determinants of these styles. A number of studies explored the idea that individual differences in identity styles are at least partly rooted in underlying differences in personality (Dollinger, 1995; Duriez, Soenens, & Beyers, 2004). Apart from this, the family context is also considered to contribute to the formation of identity in general and to the development of one's identity style in particular (Grotevant, 1987).

Marcia's Identity Status(1966)	Achieved	Moratorium	Foreclosed	Diffusion
Loevinger's Ego Development Model(1976)	*Post – conformist*	*Post - conformist*	*Conformist*	*Pre – conformist*
Joselsen's Women Identity Status (1987)	*Path makers*	*Searchers*	*Guardians*	*Drifters*
Berzonsky's Identity Style (1989)	*Information orientated identity style*	*Information orientated identity style*	*Normative orientated identity style*	*Diffused identity style*

Table 1.1 A Comparison between Marcia's (1966) Theory of Ego Identity Statuses and other Identity Theories

Adams & Serafini: The Identity Functions Model

A further important contribution to the identity field has been that of Adams (Adams & Marshall, 1996; Serafini & Adams, 2002), focusing on the "functions" of identity. Drawing upon the Eriksonian notion that identity fulfills a self-regulatory function, Adams and Marshall (1996) proposed a model including five identity functions.

1. First, identity provides individuals with a sense of structure with which to understand self-relevant information.

2. Second, identity provides a sense of consistency, coherence, and harmony between and among one's chosen values, beliefs, and commitments (Dunkel, 2005).

3. Third, identity provides individuals with a future orientation and with a sense of continuity among past, present, and future (Luyckx, Lens, Smits, & Goossens, 2010).

4. Fourth, identity offers "goals" and direction through commitments and values chosen by individuals (McGregor & Little, 1998).

5. Finally, identity provides a sense of personal control, free will, or agency that enables active self-regulation in the process of setting and achieving goals, moving toward future plans, and processing experiences in ways that are self-relevant (Côté & Levine, 2002).

These identity functions focus on the outcomes of successful and mature identity development, thus mapping onto Erikson's premise of an "optimal identity" (1968). All five identity functions have been consistently positively related to the achieved identity status (Serafini, 2007; Serafini &Adams, 2002). Furthermore, an unpublished study conducted with Canadian youth (Serafini, 2008) showed some preliminary evidence about links between identity functions and identity styles, indicating that identity functions are positively related to both information-oriented and normative identity styles, and negatively related to the diffuse-avoidant identity style.

Luyckx: Four Dimensional Model of Identity

In one of the most recent extensions of the identity status model, Luyckx, Goossens, and Soenens (2005) differentiated exploration and commitment each into two separate dimensions -

Exploration in Breadth was viewed as the gathering of information about different identity alternatives to guide the formation of commitments. It is the degree to which adolescents search for different alternatives with respect to their goals, values, and beliefs before making commitments.

Commitment Making was viewed as the actual making of choices. It the degree to which adolescents has made choices about important identity-relevant issues. Exploration in breadth and commitment making represent the dimensions proposed by Marcia (1966) and refined by others (Grotevant, 1987).

Exploration in Depth was viewed as the gathering of information about current choices. Thus it is the degree to which these commitments resemble the internal standards upheld by the individual.

Identification with Commitment was viewed as the degree of identification with those choices. It is the degree to which adolescents feel certain about, can identify with, and internalize their choices (i.e., identification with commitment) is also an important component of identity formation

Later, Luyckx et al. (2007) added a fifth dimension *ruminative exploration* which is labeled as maladaptive exploration. Ruminative exploration is positively related to distress and to self-rumination.

The **Achievement** cluster was characterized by high scores on all four dimensions.

The **Foreclosure** cluster was characterized by low scores on exploration in breadth, high scores on commitment making, and moderate to high scores on exploration in depth and identification with commitment. Apparently,

27

achievement and foreclosure were not only distinguished on the exploration dimensions; identification with commitment was also substantially higher in achievement than in foreclosure, probably as an indication of the integrated and personalized sense of identity characteristic of the Achievement status.

The **Moratorium** cluster scored low on both commitment dimensions, high on exploration in breadth, and moderately high on exploration in depth. The somewhat lower score for exploration in depth (as compared to exploration in breadth) might indicate that current tentative commitments were not as actively explored as different identity alternatives were.

Both **Carefree Diffusion** and **Diffused Diffusion** scored low on exploration in depth and identification with commitment. Marcia (1976, 1989) distinguished between the Diffused and carefree diffusion Status to indicate that there are both healthy and pathological aspects to this status (Waterman, 1992). He described the adolescent in the latter status as someone who is untroubled by the absence of strong commitments. Archer and Waterman (1990) made a distinction between similar identity subgroups in the diffusion status, that is, apathetic and commitment-avoiding individuals. Whereas the former display an "I don't care" attitude to mask an underlying uncertainty or insecurity, the latter rather enjoy their current lack of commitments. Some individuals may see their current lack of commitment as a hiatus (Diffused Diffusion), whereas others may be truly unconcerned about life (Carefree Diffusion).

Ruminative Moratorium, by contrast, would be characterized by an additional high score on ruminative exploration and, consequently, would reflect a less adaptive form of moratorium. So, by including ruminative exploration as an additional identity dimension have emerged in which progressive identity development would be hampered by higher levels of rumination and uncertainty.

Dimension	Achieve-ment	Foreclosure	Moratorium	Ruminative Moratorium	Carefree Diffusion	Diffused Diffusion
Commitment making	*High*	*High*	*Low to moderate*	*Low to moderate*	*Low*	*Low*
Identification with commitment	*High*	*High*	*Low to moderate*	*Low to moderate*	*Low*	*Low*
Exploration in breadth	*High*	*High*	*High*	*High*	*Low to moderate*	*Low to moderate*
Exploration in depth	*Low*	*Low*	*Moderate to high*	*Moderate to high*	*Low to moderate*	*Low to moderate*
Ruminative exploration	*Low*	*Low*	*Low*	*High*	*Low to moderate*	*High*

Table 1.2 Luyckx Four Dimensional Model of Identity (2005, 2007)

Meeus - Crocetti: Three Dimensional Model of Identity

Since the mid-1980s, European scholars have identified multiple forms of commitment and exploration involved in the identity formation process. Within this line of research, Meeus, Crocetti, and colleagues (Crocetti et al., 2008b; Crocetti, Schwartz, Fermani, & Meeus, 2010; Meeus et al., 2010), building upon previous work by Meeus (Meeus, 1996; Meeus et al., 1999) proposed a model that encompasses three identity dimensions:

Commitment

In-depth exploration

Reconsideration of commitment.

Commitment: It refers to the strong choices that adolescents have made with regard to various developmental domains, along with the self-confidence that they derive from these choices.

In-depth exploration: It represents the ways in which adolescents maintain their present commitments. It refers to the extent to which adolescents actively explore the commitments that they already have made by reflecting on their choices, searching for information about these commitments, and talking with others about them.

Reconsideration of commitment refers to the willingness to discard one's commitments and to search for new commitments. It also refers to the comparison of present commitments with possible alternative commitments when the present ones are no longer satisfactory.

The Meeus-Crocetti model assumes that identity is formed in a process of continuous interplay between commitment, in-depth exploration, and reconsideration. It also holds that individuals enter adolescence with a set of commitments of at least minimal strength in important ideological and interpersonal identity domains, and that adolescents do not begin the identity development process with a ''blank slate.'' The initial commitments build upon the ways in which adolescents have resolved the earlier Eriksonian psychosocial crises during childhood, and have developed the ego strengths of hope, will, purpose and competence (Erikson, 1968). During adolescence, individuals manage their commitments in two ways, namely through in-depth exploration and through reconsideration. In-depth exploration is a process whereby individuals continuously monitor present commitments, which serves the functions of making them more conscious and maintaining them. Reconsideration is the process of comparing present commitments with alternative ones, and deciding whether they need to be changed. The Meeus-Crocetti model, therefore, focuses on the dynamic between certainty (exploration in depth) and uncertainty (reconsideration).

Cluster-analytic work using these three dimensions has indicated that youth can be categorized into five identity statuses, four of which resemble Marcia's original identity statuses (with caveat that foreclosure is relabeled "early closure" by Meeus et al., 2010). These studies have also extracted a fifth status, labeled searching moratorium, which represents a variant of Marcia's moratorium status (Crocetti et al., 2008a; Meeus et al., 2010) and involves revising one's current commitments. According to Meeus et al.'s conceptualization,

> **The achieved status** consists of individuals who score high on commitment and in-depth exploration, but low on reconsideration of commitment.
>
> **The early closure status** represents individuals with moderately high scores on commitment and low scores on both in-depth exploration and reconsideration of commitment
>
> **The moratorium status** consists of individuals who score low on commitment, moderately on in depth exploration and high on reconsideration of commitment.
>
> **The diffusion status** represents individuals with low scores on all three dimensions.
>
> **The searching moratorium status** is comprised of individuals high on all three dimensions. Therefore, the two moratorium statuses differ in terms of the base from which reconsideration is attempted: youth in the "classical" moratorium status are unsatisfied with their current commitments and are

31

evaluating alternatives in the service of making identity-related commitments; whereas their counterparts in the "searching moratorium" status are seeking to revise commitments that have already been enacted, and are able to do so from the secure base provided by these commitment.

Identity Status	Dimensions		
	Commitment	In-depth Exploration	Reconsideration of Commitment
Achieved	High	*High*	*Low*
Early closure	*High*	*Low*	*Low*
Moratorium	*Low*	*Moderately low*	*High*
Diffusion	*Low*	*Low*	*Low*
Searching moratorium	*High*	*High*	*High*

Table 1.3 Outline of Three Dimensional Model of Identity

Studies have consistently indicated that these identity statuses could be empirically extracted in large community samples of both Dutch (Crocetti et al., 2008a; Meeus et al., 2010) and Italian (Crocetti, Schwartz, Fermani, Klimstra, & Meeus, 2012) adolescents, in ethnic minority groups (Crocetti, Fermani, Pojaghi, & Meeus, 2011; Crocetti et al., 2008a), as well as in juvenile delinquents and clinically referred youth (Klimstra et al., 2011).

IDENTITY DIFFUSION / DIFFUSED IDENTITY

Diffused identity status is one among the four identity status given by Marcia. It characterizes low exploration and low commitment. It is viewed as a lack of integration of the concept of self and significant others. This results in a loss of capacity for self-definition and commitment to values, goals, or relationships, and a painful sense of incoherence. This is often observed as "an inability to integrate or even perceive contradictions. Diffusions come in a variety of styles, all having in common a weak or non-existent exploratory period and an inability to make definite commitments. Following are their characteristics:

Personality traits:

Diffuse individuals have shown low levels of autonomy, self-esteem, and identity (Cramer, 1997; Marcia, 1966).

They do not have firm identity-defining commitments and not interested in making them, they seem content to "go where the wind blows" or wherever circumstances push them. They have demonstrated the lowest sense of personal integrative continuity over time (Berzonsky, Rice & Neimeyer, 1991).

They are also most likely to have difficulties in adapting to a university environment (Berzonsky and Kuk, 2000) and are most likely to be shy (Hamer & Bruch, 1994). Adams et al. (1984) found them to be most influenced by peer pressures toward conformity, compared with other identity statuses.

They were also the most self-focused of all identity statuses on a task that required them to estimate being the focus of others' attention (Adams, Abraham, & Markstrom, 1987). Grandiose self-expression as well as disagreeableness has been associated with the identity diffusion status (Blustein & Palladino, 1992; Clancy & Dollinger, 1993).

They have also shown high levels of neuroticism (along with the moratoriums) and lowest levels of conscientiousness (Clancy & Dollinger, 1993). Taken together, these findings suggest impaired psychosocial development for the late adolescent diffuse individual.

Cognitive traits:

The adolescent diffuse either rely on intuitive or dependent styles of decision-making or show an absence of systematic approaches to solving problems (Blustein & Phillips, 1990).

A diffuse/avoidant orientation to identity construction has been associated with the diffusion identity status (Berzonsky, 1990).

This social cognitive style is marked by procrastination and defensive avoidance of issues, as well as reliance on an external locus of control.

They have demonstrated preconventional, conventional, or generally low levels of moral reasoning (Podd, 1972; Skoe & Marcia, 1991).

Conformist or pre-conformist levels of ego development have also characterized the identity diffuse and foreclosed (Ginsburg & Orlofsky, 1981).

Diffusions have also scored highest of all the identity statuses on a measure of hopelessness (Selles, Markstrom- Adams, & Adams, 1994).

Interpersonal relations:

Diffusions have reported distant or rejecting caretakers or low level of attachment to parents (Campbell, Adams, & Dobson, 1984; Josselson, 1987). In addition, communication patterns have often been inconsistent.

Memories of diffusions regarding their families have carried themes of a wistful quality, wishing for strong adults to care and set guidelines (Josselson, 1987).

In terms of social relationships, they have been most likely to use bribes and deception to exert influence on others compared with the other identity statuses (Read, Adams, & Dobson, 1984).

They are most likely to be isolated or stereotyped in their styles of intimacy with others (Orlofsky, Marcia, & Lesser, 1973). In other words, they either have established no close relationships, or tend to have relationships focused on very superficial issues.

Relationship with other personality and behavioral disorders:

According to Kernberg (1985), an incompletely integrated identity may additionally manifest in chronic emptiness, contrary behavior and superficiality or in other signs of weak ego-strength like poor anxiety tolerance and impulse control.

Identity development can be described as a continuum with identity diffusion (incoherent self-image, self-fragmentation) at one end and an integrated personal identity at the other end. Overall, identity diffusion is a core element of the "borderline personality organization" (Kernberg, 1985) and is viewed as the basis for subsequent personality pathology, leading to a broad spectrum of maladaptive and dysfunctional behaviors (Marcia, 2006).

Various studies revealed that the degree of identity diffusion could therefore be considered to be a dimension of BPD or an expression of the clinical severity. Identity diffusion could be regarded as a specific stable feature of patients with BPD (Mayer, 2005), of patients with severe personality disorders in general

(Livesley, Jang, 2005) or like other psychopathological items as a feature of a severely psychopathological state.

Identity diffused status are relatively high consumers of beer. Thus it shows that those who are lower on the ego identity scale are likely to use drug/alcohol disengagement as a coping strategy. Welton & Houser (1997) found drug abstainers to be more foreclosed but not less identity achieved than drug experimenters. Identity diffusion scores suggested these individuals were most likely to be abusers of drugs, which indicates this may be used as a coping strategy. Welton & Houser (1997) interpret these results to be a consequence of an environment in which children are encouraged to make their own decisions about values while being in a culture that emphasizes freedom without limits. This brings about a greater sense of isolation which makes the identity process more difficult and creates the need for a challenge, which may be manifested in drug experimentation.

Identity diffusion is generally considered the least mature and least complex status, reflecting apathy and lack of concern about directing one's present and future life. Individuals who remain Diffused beyond early or middle adolescence are prone to drug abuse, risky sexual behavior, and academic failure (Jones and Hartmann, 1988; Jones, 1992, 1994; White, 2000).

Identity diffusion is characterized by terms such as fragmentation, boundary confusion, and lack of cohesion in the subjective experience of self. It is distinguished from the typical identity crisis of adolescents, in that adolescents, although involved in intense conflicts and confused about the attitudes of significant others to themselves, have a clear sense of the issues and their conflictual nature and are able to describe their own personality as well as the significant others with whom they enter into conflict in an appropriate, realistic and integrated way. Thus, identity disturbance or identity diffusion is conceptualized by a lack of differentiated and integrated representations of self and others, the lack of long-term goals, negative self-image and the lack of a sense of continuity in self-perception over time (Marcia, 2006; Fonagy, Gergely: Jurist, and Target, 2002; Westen, Betan, Defife, 2011; Crick, Murray, Woods, 2005; Poreh, Rawlings, Claridge, Freeman, Faulkner, Shelton, 2006).

CORRELATES OF IDENTITY DIFFUSION

Contemporary researches revealed that development of an individual's identity profoundly shaped by various psycho-social factors. Identity development is shaped profoundly by macro-level factors such as culture (Taylor & Oskay, 1995), gender roles (Lewis, 2003), and history (Burkitt, 2011). Identity is also likely to be shaped by individual-difference characteristics such as temperament, attribution style, etc.

RESILIENCE

Resilience refers to the process of overcoming the negative effects of risk exposure, coping successfully with traumatic experiences, and avoiding the negative trajectories associated with risks. The basic element for resilience is that there should be risk and protective factors available which can get an optimistic result or can decrease negative result. The theory of resilience basically focuses on youth's exposure to risk on the strength instead of weakness and also on understanding healthy growth even with the presence of risk.

According to **Rutter (1990),** resilience refers to the positive adaptation in the faceof stress or trauma. Resilience is inherent in the way human beings deal with life changes and other complex life situations.

Luthar and Cicchetti (2000) defined resilience as a relatively good outcome even though an individual may experience situations that have been shown to carry significant risk for developing psychopathology.

Ungar (2004) defined resilience as "the outcome from negotiations between individuals and their environments for the resources to define themselves as healthy amidst conditions collectively viewed as adverse".

Thus, resilience is the process of adapting well in the face of adversity, trauma, tragedy, threats or even significant sources of stress such as family and relationships problems, serious health problems or workplace and financial stressors. It means bouncing back from the difficult experiences. Resilience thus refers to the concept that even in situations of multiple risks to an individual's development, there are certain qualities within the individual or his/her environment that allows him/her to deal with these risks and thrive in spite of them (Engle et.al, 1996). Two critical conditions are inferred within the concept –

the person should have been/be exposed to significant threat(s) or to severe adversity.

the person should achieve positive adaptation despite major assaults on the developmental process (Smokowski, Reynolds & Bezruczko, 1999).

The protective factors that enable adolescents to reduce or eliminate the harmful effect of risk can be called as either asset or resources. Assets can be those helpful factors that are present inside an individual like competency, stress dealing skills and self-efficacy. The other category is of resources, those helpful factors that are available in outer environment like resilience by parents, parental support, and community role in developing adolescent in a positive way. Resources focus on the social environmental influences on individual's health and growth, that places resilience theory in a more ecological context and moves away from conceptualizations of resilience as a static, individual trait. It also states that resources can be a focus of change to enable youth deal with the risk and discourage harmful results. For e.g. individuals developing in financial deficiency may be at a risk of having variety of negative result. Various professionals in the field of resilience have stated that along with these issues many individuals growing in financial deficit show positive result. They may have variety of protective factors like good self-esteem or the availability of an adult guide that enables them to eliminate the harmful result related to poverty. Assets or resources to get over the risk indicated resilience as a process. Research professionals have also stated resilience as a result when they indicate a person as resilient when he/she has come out of the risk successfully.

The base of resilience covers the psychological resources like flexible self-concept that allow individuals to alter the fundamental of their self-definition as per the changing conditions, a sense of autonomy, self-direction, environmental mastery and competency. Ann Masten (2001) review of relevant research suggests that resilience is best characterized as ordinary magic. She concludes that resilience in the face of challenge is quite common and does not arise from superhuman effort and abilities.

Resilience is quite common because human protective systems are part of nearly everyone's life. Research points again and again to the same number of factors that serve as protective functions. On the basis of the research on children and youth, Masten and Reed (2002) have divided protective factors in 3 groups: those within the child, within the family and within the community.

Protective factors within the child include:

Good intellect and abilities to solve problem.

A trouble free temperament and a flexible personality.

A positive self-image and personal effectiveness.

A positive viewpoint

Ability to handle emotions and impulses

Individual talents that is valued by the individual and by his or her culture.

A good sense of humor.

Protective factors within the family covers:

Close relationship with parents or other basic care givers.

Healthy and supportive parenting that states clear demands and rules.

An emotionally positive family with very less conflict among parents.

Structured and organized home environment.

Parents who give time to their child's education.

Parents with sufficient finances.

Protective factors within the community covers:

Attending a decent school.

Taking part in social organizations in the school and community.

Living in a neighborhood of involved and care giving people who deals with problems and enhance community spirits.

Living in a part neighborhood.

Easy availability of competent and responsive emergency, public health and social service.

It encompasses the psychological damage and the enduring strength that can result from struggling with hardship. These strengths include resiliencies such as: insight, independence, relationships, initiative, creativity, humor, and morality. For each of the resiliencies there are three developmental phases: child, adolescent, and adult. In children, resiliencies appear as unformed and not associated with a goal. In adolescents, these behaviors sharpen and become deliberate. In adults, they expand and have more depth and become a continuing part of the self (Project Resilience, version current November 11, 1999). Some researchers suggest that the first ten years of a child's life are most favorable for developing strong coping skills, but there is no set timeline for finding strength and resiliency. People who cope well with adversity are able to ask for help from others if they do not have a strong family support system. Setting goals and planning for the future is also a strong factor in dealing with adversity. Believing in oneself and recognizing one's strengths is important; you give yourself value and surround yourself with things that help you stabilize. Finally, it is essential to actually recognize one's own strengths (Blum, 1998).

Identity development is significantly influenced by the environmental and psychological dynamics experienced during an individual's lifetime, most notably during adolescence. The process of identity development takes place as an individual learns to cope with new challenges and adopts values through which he/she is able to navigate through life and become an established part of his or her social environment. By the time an individual has reached adulthood, s/he will have developed his or her general framework for interacting with the environment and coping with stress. An individual's identity can influence his or her responses to stressful experiences in a no. of ways. For example, one's identity status or level of identity achievement can influence one's social cognitive orientation – how one processes problems and makes decisions. (Berzonsky, 1988, 1989b). It has been shown that individuals who have not developed a clear sense of identity tend to procrastinate and avoid dealing with problems and making decisions. On the other hand, individuals who have achieved a clear sense of identity tend to effort fully seek out and evaluate relevant information in their problem solving and decision making processes (Berzonsky, 1992). Identity may also play a role in how an individual reacts emotionally to stress. Research has shown that individuals who have achieved a clear sense of identity are more likely to experience debilitating emotional states such as anxiety and depression. As the coping process involves some management of the emotional distress that accompanies stressful events (Eisenberg, Fabes & Guthie, 1997), an individual's identity may be predictive of how an individual regulates his or her emotions in response to these stressors.

WELL-BEING

The history of well-being dates back to 1961 when the term 'wellness' was coined and defined as an integrated method of functioning, which is oriented toward maximizing the potential, of which the individual is capable. This is the fact that healthy person can be adjusted in the society. Health simply does not mean a good state of health or free from diseases, but also a psychological well-being of an individual. Well-being requires harmony between mind and body. It implies a sense of balance and ease with the pressures in a person's life. There is no under-stimulation and no excessive negative stress; above all, there is a sense of control over one's destiny.

Sushrutha, a prominent proponent of the system of Indian medicine defines it as state characterized by a feeling of spiritual, physical and mental well-being (Prasanna Atma Indirayamana). Thus well-being is a conglomeration of several dimensions of aspects psychological, spiritual, social and physical.

The Oxford English Dictionary (Simpson and Weiner, 1989) states well-being as, "A state of being or doing well in life, happy, healthy or prosperous condition; moral or physical welfare". It is a dynamic process, which involves the striving for balance and integration in one's life, and refining skills, rethinking previous beliefs and stances towards issues as appropriate.

The concept of wellbeing is defined and explained in a variety of ways in literature. It has been primarily viewed from an intra-personal perspective, something that happens within an individual. Ryff and Singer (1998) used the term „human flourishing" and Felce & Perry (1995) call it a comprising of objective descriptors and subjective evaluations of physical, material, social and emotional well-being. Ryan and Deci (2000, 2001) suggests that humans have three basic psychological needs; competence, autonomy, and relatedness. The satisfaction of these needs lead to both subjective well-being (increased pleasure and happiness) and psychological well-being. Waterman (2008) reviews three specific variants of well-being:

(a) *Subjective well-being*, which refers to self-esteem, life satisfaction, and the absence of anxiety and depressive symptoms (Diener, 2006);

(b) *Psychological well-being*, which refers to a sense of mastery over one's life tasks (e.g., satisfying relationships, a comfortable school or work environment; Ryff & Singer, 2008);

(c) *Eudemonic well-being*, which refers to having discovered one's calling and living in accordance with one's highest potentials (Waterman et al., 2010).

Components of psychological well-being

Ryff and Keyes (1995) identified six concepts associated with psychological well-being namely self-acceptance, *autonomy, personal growth, environmental mastery, purpose in life and positive relations.*

Self-acceptance - This is denned as a central feature of well - being as well as a characteristic of self-actualization, optimal functioning, and maturity. Life span theories also emphasize acceptance of self and of one's past life. Thus, holding positive attitudes toward oneself emerges as a central characteristic of positive psychological functioning.

Autonomy- It involves self-determination, independence, control and the regulation of behavior from within. The fully functioning person is also described as having an internal locus of evaluation, whereby one does not look to others for approval, but evaluates oneself by personal standards. Individuation is seen to involve a deliverance from convention, in which the person no longer clings to the collective fears, beliefs, and laws of the masses.

Personal growth - It is associated with people who show autonomous functioning. A fully functioning person is described as having an internal locus of evaluation and evaluation of the self by personal standards instead of clings to the collective fears, beliefs and the laws of the masses. Optimal psychological functioning requires not only that one achieve the prior characteristics, but also that one continue to develop one's potential, to grow and expand as a person. The need to actualize oneself and realize one's potentialities is central to the clinical perspectives on personal growth. Openness to experience, for example, is a key characteristic of the fully functioning person. Such an individual is continually developing and becoming, rather than achieving a fixed state wherein all problems are solved. Life span theories also give explicit emphasis to continued growth and the confronting of new challenges or tasks at different periods of life.

Environmental mastery – It is associated with the individual's ability to choose or create environments suitable to his or her psychic conditions. Maturity is seen to require participation in a significant sphere of activity outside of self. Life span development is also described as requiring the ability to manipulate and control complex environments. These theories emphasize one's ability to advance in the world and change it through physical or mental activities. Successful aging also emphasizes the extent to which the individual takes advantage of environmental opportunity. These combined perspectives suggest that active participation in and mastery of environment is important ingredients of an integrated framework of positive psychological functioning.

Purpose in Life - *It* is also considered to be an important ingredient in one's life; the beliefs that give one the feeling there is purpose in and meaning to life. The definition of maturity also emphasizes a clear comprehension of life's purpose, a sense of directedness, and intentionality. Psychological well-being include beliefs that give one the feeling there is purpose in and meaning to life. It includes a clear comprehension of life's purpose, a sense of directedness, and intentionality. An individual must be productive and creative and achieving emotional integration in later life. Thus, one who functions positively has goals, intentions, and a sense of direction, all of which contribute to the feeling that life is meaningful

Positive Relations with Others – Having positive relations with others and the ability to love is viewed as the central component of mental health. Self-actualizes are described as having strong feelings of empathy and affection for all human beings and as being capable of great love, deeper friendship, and positive identification with others. It emphasizes on the importance of warm, trusting interpersonal relations and the ability to love. It also includes strong feelings of empathy and affection for all human beings and as being capable of greater love, deeper friendship, and more complete identification with others. The importance of positive relations with others is repeatedly stressed in these conceptions of psychological wellbeing.

In terms of identity status, Waterman (2007) found that a measure of achievement was positively related, and a measure of diffusion was negatively related, to all three forms of well-being. Waterman (2007) argues that the exploration of a variety of possibilities increases the likelihood to identify resolutions to identity issues consistent with personal talents and needs but also to yield greater information about benefits and costs of possible alternatives. Thus, individuals are more likely to succeed when pursuing such self-congruent and informed commitments and, finally, to enjoy higher levels of well-being. A low level of identity resulted in a lower level of psychological well – being. According to St. Louis and Liem (2005) adolescents with an achieved identity seem to have higher self-esteem than youths in other identity statuses. Findings of Meeus (1999) accentuated the importance of identity commitment which was associated with personal well-being measures. The sequence of identity statuses from low to high psychological well-being was moratorium, diffusion, foreclosure and achievement.

PARENTING STYLE

A parenting style is a psychological construct representing standard strategies that parents use in their child rearing. Parenting style is affected by both parents and children's temperaments and is largely based on the influence of one's own parents and culture. Identity development involves an active exploration of and a relatively firm commitment to individually specific morals, viewpoints, and aspirations in life (Erikson, 1968). Parents can either help or hinder this process through their childrearing behaviors (Adams, Dyk, & Benisisnion, 1990).

Darling & Steinberg define parenting style as "a constellation of attitudes toward the child that are communicated to the child and that, taken together, create an emotional climate in which the parents' behaviors are expressed" (1993, p 488). Parenting style is distinguished from parenting practices, in that parenting practices are directed towards particular goals--encouraging academic achievement, for example--while parenting style refers to the overall emotional climate in which particular parent: child interactions occur. It is an interaction between parents and child that can help children acquire some positive skills. The skills included problem solving skill, language and impulse control, proper social interaction and expectations. These skills can reduce the chance of adolescents engage in maladaptive behavior such as aggressive behavior. Early work towards parenting style by **Diane Baumrind** (1967, 1971) classified parents have three parenting styles, which are authoritative, authoritarian, and indulgent-permissive based on the inclusion or exclusion of two dimensions (responsiveness and demandingness).

a) **Responsiveness** - It can be described as the degree to which parents promote autonomy and self-assertiveness in their children. Responsiveness further entails that parents are familiar with and accommodating towards their children's developmental needs. For example, parents are warm and supportive of adolescents' search for autonomy (Baumrind, 1966, 2005). Thus, support of autonomy is viewed as encouragement, acceptance, and supportiveness towards adolescents' developmental processes (Ryan, Jorm & Lubman, 2010). Therefore, responsiveness can be defined as parents' awareness of their adolescents' developmental needs and willingness to provide support, love, and admiration (Shaffer, 2002).

b) **Demandingness** - It is explained as the demands and limits parents set for their children (Baumrind, 1966). Demandingness can be explained further as how restrictive and challenging parents are towards their children (Shaffer, 2002). Sigelman and Rider (2009) suggest that demandingness is the amount of control and monitoring practiced by parents over their children's decision-making processes. Parental control and monitoring are defined as the enforcement of parental rules and attentiveness to children's daily activities (Kwon & Wickrama,

2013). Thus, demanding parents set rules, expect their children to obey the rules without questioning them, and monitor compliance (Shaffer, 2002).

Grouping the degree of responsiveness and demandingness creates the three parenting styles, namely authoritarian, authoritative, and permissive (Baumrind, 2005). Each of the three parenting styles is complex and provides a unique description of the parenting behaviour with which it is associated (Baumrind, 1966, 1971, 2005; Sharma, Sharma, & Yadava, 2011).

Dimensions	Authoritative	Authoritative	Permissive
Responsiveness	High	Low	High
Demandingness	High	High	Low

Table 1.4 Baumrind's (1966, 1991, 2005) Parenting Styles

Authoritarian parenting style - Prototypic authoritarian parents are generally described by their "attempts to shape, control, and evaluate behavior and attitudes in accordance with a set standard of conduct" (Baumrind, 1968). They value obedience and conformity, and tend to favor punitive and forceful measures of discipline. Authoritarian parents also tend not to encourage independence and their style of parenting restricts the child's autonomy.

Authoritative parenting style – Authoritative parents encourage autonomy but with clear standards of conduct. They are warm and nurturing to their children yet apply firm control in a rational, issue-oriented manner that allows for a verbal give and take (Baumrind, 1968). Both the authoritative and authoritarian styles of parenting are high on demandingness, which refers to the degree to which the parent expects and demands mature, responsible behavior from the child, but differ on the extent of parental responsiveness, which refers to the degree to which the parent responds to the child's needs in an accepting, supportive manner (Maccoby & Martin, 1983).

Permissive parenting style - A prototypic indulgent parent adopts a permissive style, in which parents are highly involved with their children but place very few controls and are more passive in their limited disciplinary actions. Parents are responsive but not demanding. They are nurturing and accepting but do not require children to regulate themselves or behave appropriately.

Expanding upon Baumrind's (1971) classifications of parenting patterns, Maccoby and Martin (1983) identified neglectful or uninvolved style of parenting. Uninvolved parents are neither demanding nor responsive. These parents are extremely uninvolved and are indifferent with their children.If parenting guides adolescents along a particular trajectory, then a neglectful style of parenting is least likely to assist adolescents in resolving their identity crisis. This claim was indirectly investigated by Steinberg et al. (1991) who found that "compared with their counterparts from non-authoritative homes, authoritatively reared adolescents earn higher grades in school, are more self-reliant, report less psychological distress, and are less involved in delinquent activity" . Conversely, an authoritarian maternal parenting style was associated with an elevated level of conduct problems (Forehand & Nousiainen, 1993). Avoidant parents who have a high conflict level with their adolescent espouse a firm and non-accepting parenting style that negatively affects identity development (Reis & Youniss, 2004). Adolescents who have explored and committed to an identity experienced more openness, less problems, and better overall communication with both their parents, as compared to an unachieved identity group (Bhushan & Shirali, 1992). Effective parenting transcends the home environment and allows for achievement in contexts outside of the family, such as in school. Parents have the opportunity to facilitate or impede academic achievement, which is just one aspect of an ideological identity, through their parenting style. The warmth, acceptance, and firmness of authoritative parents have a significant impact on school performance and engagement, such that adolescents from authoritative homes perform better in school and have stronger school engagement than their peers from homes with other parenting styles (Steinberg et al., 1992) Research since the mid-1970s utilizing these parenting styles has demonstrated that authoritative parenting is optimal, as compared to authoritarian or permissive styles, for positive outcomes to various psychosocial issues associated with adolescence (Steinberg, 2001).

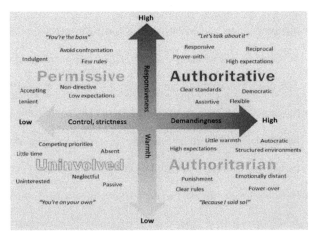

Fig 1.2 Dimensions of Parenting and Parenting styles
Source: Sustaining Community (2015)

Adams et al. (1990) integrated several parenting theories to derive generalizations of parental characteristics that facilitate or impede their adolescent's identity development. The more emotionally facilitative behaviors of parents are associated with warmth, companionship, and acceptance. The more conduct-oriented factors that facilitate identity development involve setting reasonable behavioral standards, independence training, acceptance of others' perspectives, and disciplined compliance to behavioral expectations. Parents who encourage self-expression, the acceptance of unique viewpoints, and respect for others' perspectives positively impact identity exploration and commitment. Emotionally-based parenting practices that inhibit adolescent identity development include hostility, restrictiveness, emotional distance, or perceived rejection. High frequencies of parental binding behaviors, systemic rigidity, or chaos in the family's ability to adjust to the child's growth toward maturity greatly impede the identity processes. These emotionally-based and conduct-oriented factors that either help or hinder adolescents in their identity crisis are descriptive of the previously mentioned patterns of parenting.

Thus identity diffusion is found to be a status of no achievement where an individual fails to resolve crises related to various domains of his/her life. Various models and researches done on identity status paradigm and its expansion shed light on the interplay of psycho-social factors influencing one's identity development.

ATTRIBUTION STYLE

'Attribution style' or 'Explanatory Style' refers to how people explain the events of their life. Attribution Theory by Weiner proposes that the way in which individuals perceive or judge why an event occurs, and the allocation of responsibility, guides subsequent behavior (Weiner, 1972). This theory has predominantly been studied within the domains of achievement, motivation and emotion (Weiner, 1985). In 1985, Weiner proposed that the perceived causes of events have three common properties: locus, stability and controllability. Attribution theory distinguishes between the individual themselves (locus) and their ability to exert control (controllability). This theory presents a process by which explanations of events have been shown to impact on an individual's affectivity and behavior, and has applied this to help explain theories of motivation, achievement and learning. Furthermore, the theory also pertains that the way in which events are explained can be altered by the individual in order to increase individual success (Weiner, 1985). In this way, it also provides support for the concept that how people attribute causes to events in their lives will impact upon their future expectancies, or dispositional optimism (Scheier & Carver, 1985).

DIMENSION	EXPLAINATION
Locus	Refers to whether the cause of an event is internal (because of the individual) or external (due to the environment).
Stability	Refers to whether the causal factor fluctuates or is it always the same.
Controllability	This dimension was created in order to account for volitional controllability. It refers to whether the cause of an event is perceived as being controllable or not.

Table 1.5   The three dimensions of the causal structure of the Attribution Theory as proposed by Weiner (1985)

EXPLANATORY STYLE

Explanatory style refers to the ways in which people routinely think about the causes of events in their lives. The terms optimism and pessimism have been applied to distinguish between different explanatory styles (Revich & Gillham, 2003). Seligman (2006) suggested explanatory style stems directly from an individual's view of their place in the world and is a habit of thought, learned throughout childhood and adolescence. "It is the hallmark of whether you are an optimist or a pessimist" (Seligman, 2006). The construct of explanatory style stems from the Reformulated Learned Helplessness Theory (RLHT: Abramson et al., 1978) which proposes that the attributions an individual makes can be measured across three crucial dimensions that have been labelled as the „three Ps" (Seligman, 2006). These dimensions are portrayed in Table given below.

DIMENSION	EXPLAINATION	EXAMPLE
Permanence *(Stable to unstable)*	Whether the attribution is made to a cause which is always going to be present (stable) or a cause which is present just that time (unstable).	People who give up easily believe the causes of bad events to be permanent: e.g. "pupils never listen", as opposed to "they're just distracted today".
Personalization *(Internal to external)*	Whether the cause of the event is internal, attributed to the individual themselves, or external, attributed to causes outside the individual.	Individuals can blame themselves for events or other people or circumstances: e.g. "I'm a boring teacher" as opposed to "It's nearly lunchtime and the pupils are hungry".
Pervasiveness *(Global or specific)*	Whether the cause of the event is believed to influence just the situation in question (specific) or whether it influences all other parts of the individual's life (global).	When something bad happens at work, some people can put it in a box and forget about it when they go home, whilst others will let it affect their mood and behavior for the rest of the day.

Table 1.6 The Three Dimensions of Explanatory Style (Seligman, 2006)

According to Rotter, behavior can be predicted from individual's values, expectations, and the situation in which they find themselves. Locus of control is a type of expectation regarding how much control individuals feel they have over what occurs in a situation. Rotter realized that individuals" expectations affect their behavior. People vary in the extent to which they perceive control.

Internal locus of control: Some have a general propensity to perceive control. They consider themselves responsible for the success and failure in their life.

External locus of control: Some feel that what happens in life is largely outside of their control, determined by other people or circumstances.

Additionally, locus of control describes the degree to which a person considers events to be internally or externally controlled (Rotter, 1971).Research on a possible link between identity and locus of control grew from investigations that showed youth became more internal in their locus of control as they matured (Matteson, 1977). Several researchers also found two of the most common findings are that the identity achieved score high on the internal locus of control scale (and low on the external locus of control), and that the identity diffuse score low on the internal control scale (and high on the external locus of control) (Abraham, 1983; Adelberg, 1986).diffused individuals look to others for their self-definition.

DECISION MAKING STYLES

Adolescents increasingly face with making many important life decisions influencing their future. The decision making skills should help the adolescents to better manage difficult decision situations (D'Zurilla & Chang, 1995; Mann, Harmoni & Power,

1989). Many researchers have stated that decision making skills should be taught routinely during adolescence, at an age when vital choices are already being made (Baron, 1989; Mann, Harmoni & Power, 1989). Among researchers, there is a lack of consensus as to how decision-making styles should be conceptualized. The main point of divergence appears to be whether decision-making styles represent stable individual differences across time and situations or a more state-like quality. In support of the latter, decision-making styles have been described as fluid states, which people easily and frequently alternate among.The decision- making style refers to the unique manner in which an individual approaches, responds to, and acts in a decision-making situation (Arroba, 1977; Payne, Bettmen, & Johnson, 1993). Therefore, decision making behavior includes several individual differences. Also, an individual's career decision-making style is an important factor effecting the process and outcome of career decision-making (Gati & Asher, 2001).

Decision-making style is defined by Scott and Bruce (1995) as "the learned, habitual response pattern exhibited by an individual when confronted with a decision situation. It is not a personality trait, but a habit-based propensity to react in a certain way to a specific decision context."

Some researchers have suggested a close relationship between decision-making style and cognitive style with some suggesting decision-making style as "a subset of broader cognitive styles, defined generally as the way people deploy their intellectual abilities or the manner in which they approach cognitive tasks. While some elements of decision-making styles do appear to be "reflective of individual cognitive style" (Scott & Bruce, 1995), decision-making also represents a unique construct that should be treated as a separate dimension of one's response to decision situations and should be tested in specific contexts to further examine decision-making style as a subset or connected facet of cognitive style. To understand the construct of individual differences in career decision making, career development theorists and researchers have determined several decisional styles (Arroba, 1977; Harren, 1979; Jepsen, 1974; Johnson, 1978; Kuzgun, 2005; Scott & Bruce, 1995). Harren (1979) examined decision-making models as "conceptual frameworks for understanding how decision-makers process information and arrive at conclusions". In Harren's model, a four – stage sequence is proposed: awareness, planning, commitment, and implementation. Furthermore, Harren explained that a person's self-concept and style are influential factors in this process which establish three distinct types of decision-makers: rational, intuitive, and dependent.

Scott and Bruce Model of Decision Making Styles

Scott and Bruce (1995) expanded this model to five decision-making styles which included Harren's (1979) *rational*, *intuitive*, and *dependent* types, and added *avoidant* and *spontaneous* types.

1) **Rational style** - Rational decision-makers are described as using "a thorough search for and logical evaluation of alternatives" to make decisions. It is characterized by deliberate, emotion-free, analytic information processing. It is a strong predictor of coping ability and adjustment (Epstein et al, 1996). It is also characterized by systematic and planful strategies with a clear future orientation. The rational decision- makers accept responsibility for choice that is derived from

an internal locus of control and are active, deliberate and logical (Harren 1979; Kuzgun, 2005; Rubinton, 1980).

2) **Intuitive style** - Intuitive decision-makers rely "hunches and feelings" as their primary method of making decisions. It is characterized by automatic, quick, emotion-based information processing. Intuitive thinking style is associated with the use of heuristics. This style is a stronger predictor of heuristic processing and is associated with irrational forms of coping, such as the use of superstitions (Epstein et al., 1996). It is characterized by the reliance on inner experience, fantasy, and a propensity to decide rapidly without much deliberation or information gathering. The intuitive decisionmakers accept responsibility for choice, but focus on emotional self- awareness, fantasy and feeling, often in impulsive manner (Harren, 1979; Kuzgun, 1995; Payne et al., 1993).

3) **Dependent style** - Dependent decision-makers engage in "a search for advice and direction from others". It involves denying responsibility for their choices and projects responsibility towards others, generally authority figures (Kuzgun, 2005).

4) **Avoidant style** - Avoidant decision-makers "attempt to avoid decision-making" altogether. They tend to avoid decision- making situations or project responsibility toward others. Indecisive persons need significantly more time when they have to make a choice (Rassin, Muris, Booster & Kolsloot, 2008), but they are also more selective and less exhaustive in their information search (Bacanli, 2006; Ferrari & Dovidio, 2000; Rassin et al., 2008).

5) **Spontaneous style** - Spontaneous decision-makers rely on a "sense of immediacy and a desire to get through the decision-making process as soon as possible".

Their choices are often dictated by immediate feelings.Together these five styles make up the General Decision-Making Style (GDMS) measure.

Marcia (1980), Miller-Tiedeman (1980), and Waterman (1985) suggested that persons at various stages of development tend to approach decisions in rather different yet predictable factions. From the ego identity perspective, the exploration and commitment processes not involve only vocational decisions, but also involve a lot general decisions related to political, friendship, and dating domains, values, beliefs, and goals. Hence, in adolescence lack of decision making competencies is correlated with the lack of knowledge of one's own abilities and present and future preferences that is necessary to work out a self-image mirroring one's own identity. It can also be assumed that the resolution of the identity crisis is largely determined by the decision-making style of the individual concerned.

CHAPTER 2

REVIEW OF LITERATURE

REVIEW OF LITERATURE

This chapter compiles and summarizes research findings related to all the variables selected for the present study. It consists of the review of research on identity status and the role of various psycho-social factors in identity diffusion along with identity intervention studies.

Identity

Identity is a complex psychosocial concept which has inspired numerous research approaches and emphasis since its first introduction by Erikson in 1950. Whereas Erikson wrote on identity in primary theoretical and clinical terms, Marcia's (1966) ego identity status paradigm was the first approach to the operationalization of identity to gain acceptance for purposes of the systematic study of identity under circumstances of normative socialization. Marcia (1993) estimated that in the first 25 years of identity research, more than 300 studies had been conducted. There is an extensive body of research literature demonstrating the discriminant validity of the identity statuses (Marcia, Waterman, Matteson, Archer & Orlofsky, 1993; Meuss, 1996). Within the past decade, however, there have been numerous efforts to broaden or reformulate the conceptualization of identity formation. Considerable research has been devoted to understanding the influences on and the consequences of the development of identity and the correlates of each identity status (Adams, Gullotta & Montemayor, 1992; Kroger, 1993; Marcia, Waterman, Matteson, Archer & Orlofsky, 1993; Waterman, 1984). Most of these efforts have built on the identity status paradigm; although they have differed in the extent to which the reconceptualizations are compatible with the original paradigm. Ego identity is a complex construct and has been researched on multiple occasions. In a meta-analysis, Jespersen, Kroger and Martinussen (2013) identified 565 empirical studies of ego identity status in relation to behavioral, developmental and personality variables. Identity has been investigated by focusing on the various dimensions of Marcia's model (Crocetti, Sica, Schwartz, Serafini & Meeus, 2012), using Berzonsky's (1989) model of identity styles, and to explore the correlation of different identity configurations (Crocetti, Scrignaro, Sica & Magrin, 2012). The present study was undertaken to evaluate the studies on Marcia's identity status paradigm by focusing the role of various psychological and social factors on identity diffusion so efforts can be taken to resolve this status. These initial studies as well as some later ones yielded a number of personality and social correlates of identity and established the identity statuses as discriminable modes of identity resolution.

Resilience

Resilience refers to pathways and patterns of positive adaptation during or following significant risk or adversity (Masten, 2011; Masten & Tellegen, 2012). It is not an attribute of the individual, but it is instead a phenomenon that is inferred based on two fundamental judgments: First, the person must be, or have been, exposed to significant risk or adversity, and second, he/she must be "doing ok" despite stress exposure. Comparative studies show that adolescents whose sense of identity is strong, and that weighed the various aspects of their occupation and ideology and arrived at conclusions remained more committed to their conclusions. They also less often underwent the pressure to conform to others, feeling less inconvenient while resisting against such pressures, thereby are more resilient. While reviewing the literature in relation to resilience and identity status, a few studies have been found.

Cramer (2000) conducted a study on 200 males and females of college students and revealed the association of Marcia's theory with ego-resiliency, self-monitoring, self-esteem· and openness to experience. His results suggested that achieved identity is strongly positively correlated to high self-esteem, low anxiety and low level of depression while negative correlation was found between identity diffusion and high levels of anxiety and depression.

Many researches were obtained linking identity with resilience where resilience was further associated with vulnerability including psychological distress, depression and anxiety and mental health. The more an adolescent enjoys mental health and resilience the sooner he or she achieves identity. Otherwise, a state of diffusion (perturbed) will occur. The adolescents who enjoy advanced identity possess a higher sense of self-esteem, and abstract thinking, and higher similarity between their real self and ideal self. They are also more advanced independent, more resilient and more tolerant against problems and difficulties. While on the other side adolescents with diffused identity status have a lower self-esteem and a less developed moral reasoning. They shoulder their responsibility with difficulty. They are impulsive having irregular thinking. They are also more susceptible to taking drugs. Their individual relationships are often perfunctory and occasional although, they generally disagree to their parent's life- styles; they are unable to invent an approach of their own. Psychological health and vulnerability indices are influenced by different levels of resilience through self-esteem, personal competence and tenacity, tolerance of negative affect, control, and spirituality (Marcia, 1966; Dyer & Guinness, 1996 & Banijamali, 1995; Berzonsky and Kuk, 2000; Cramer, 2000; Muzzafari, 2008; Haddadi & Besharat, 2010; Papy, Khagevand & Nasab, 2014).

One survey study was done by Bayazidi & Ghaderi (2012) to examine the relationship between identity style and hardiness in student. In their scientific –comparative investigation, community investigation include of Payame Noor University of Boukan in 2011-2012 educational year and a number of 230(115 girls and 115 boys) students were selected. Results show that in students was a positive and significant correlation between hardiness with informational and normative identity styles and was tow predictor for hardiness - informational and normative identity styles

Safari, Rezaei, Salmabaadi and Jeenabadi (2016) conducted a correlational study to explore the prediction of resilience on the basis of identity styles. A sample of 400 high school male students was selected for the purpose. Results showed a significant correlation between identity style and resilience. Only diffused/ avoidance style showed negative relation with resilience. This explains the negative link between diffused identity status and resilience as well.

Well being

Since the inception of the ego identity status paradigm (Marcia, 1966), an extensive body of research literature has emerged indicating that the reflective consideration of identity alternatives prior to forming personally meaningful commitments is associated with more successful psychological development and more effective psychological functioning. Correspondingly, those individuals who have not formed personally meaningful identity commitments during the stage of emerging adulthood (Arnett, 2000) appear to be delayed with respect to development across a variety of psychological dimensions and to function less effectively.

The association between identity formation and well-being has been studied primarily among adolescents. An extensive review of the relationship between the identity statuses and psychological well-being in adolescence was conducted by Meeus et al. (1999), whose findings accentuated the importance of identity commitment which was associated with personal well-being measures. It was found that achievement is related to high psychological well-being. Diffusion and moratorium reported to have low psychological well-being. A slow development of identity resulted in a lower level of well-being and effective psychological functioning. Earlier studies on identity status in relation to well-being was done by taking variables like anxiety, worry, positive and negative effect, depression and loneliness. It is well known that aforementioned variables adversely affect the wellbeing of an individual therefore these are being discussed in the review.

Authors	Identity Measures	Psychological well-being Variable	Measures	Ranking of statuses on psychological well-being A	M	F	D
Adams et al., 1984	OM-EIS	Tendency to worry negative affect tendency to worry negative affect	TAIS-subscale	4 4 3 3	2 2 3 3	2 2 3 3	2 2 3 3
Craig-Bray et al, 1988	OM-EIS	Loneliness	UCLA-loneliness scale	3.5	1.5	3.5	1.5
Kapfhammer et al., 1993	EOM-EIS	Psychiatric problems	ICD 9 revised diagnosis	4	2	2	2
Marcia 1967	ISI	Anxiety	WAS	3	1	3	3
Rotheram-Borus, 1989	OM-EIS	Obsessive behavior anxiety nervousness self-destructiveness	Youth Self Report subscales	3 3 1.5 4	1 1 1.5 1	3 3 3.5 2.5	3 3 3.5 2.5

Ranking based on reported significant between status differences. Rank 1 indicates the highest (negative) score of a status on the psychological well-being measure. If two or more statuses had the same rank, the ranks were summated and divided by the number of statuses.

Table 2.1 Relationship between Identity Status and Well-Being (Meeus, 1999)

A few longitudinal studies considering outcomes in adulthood demonstrated positive implications of early identity achievement in later well-being. Kahn, Zimmerman, Csikszentmihalyi and Getzels (1985) showed that identity achievement in arts undergraduates was predictive of happiness ratings up to 18 years later in both genders and additionally for life satisfaction in men.

Jeyakumar (2001) examined the relationship between stress, identity status and well-being in 233 young undergraduates from Canada. Identity achievers in both ideological and interpersonal domains experienced significantly greater well-being than diffusions. Ideological achievers also experienced significantly greater well-being than moratoriums. They are also negatively related to symptomatology while diffused showed correlation with physical and psychological problems. This difference in well-being in each identity status attributes to their ways of coping with stress.

Sandhu and Tung (2004; 2007) conducted their study on 400 adolescents' sample (200 boys and 200 girls). Their study revealed that well-being is positively correlated with the identity achievement and moratorium, while they found inverse correlation with the foreclosure and diffusion status. This study also reveals that adolescent's experimentation with different identity issues, or commitment to life tasks after going through an exploratory period is associated with higher well-being; whereas lack of concern about one's life tasks or premature commitment to them without self-exploration accompanies lesser well-being. Likely, framing one's own identity and knowing one's own direction in life is associated with the positive outcomes, whereas lower identity statues do not indicate positive life orientation in Indian adolescents. They also observed that identity achievement is associated with the different indices of health, adjustment and well-being, while diffusion has been reported to accompany lower well-being ranging from debilitating emotional states to psychopathology. They advised that a clear sense of long self and direction in life, along with commitment to self-chosen goals and values helps adolescents to achieve life satisfaction and adjustment, while the lacking of all these is threatening to their mental health.

Hofer et al. (2007) examined the relationship between ego identity formation (commitment statuses) and subjective well-being among student samples from Cameroon and Germany. Analyses revealed that well-being was positively related to the level of identity achievement among participants from both cultural groups. In contrast, well-being did not show a positive association with commitments to goals and values that were adopted from significant others (Foreclosure). The findings reported here for identity diffusion and moratorium should be viewed as more tentative since measures for these statuses were not employed in his study.

A study involving 217 college undergraduates was conducted by Waterman (2007) to evaluate the relationship between measures of ego identity status and three conceptions of well-being: subjective, psychological, and eudaimonic. The various measures of well-being were found to be positively correlated, mostly in the low to moderate range. The identity achievement status was positively correlated with measures of all three conceptions of well-being, while corresponding negative correlations were obtained for identity diffusion scores. The correlations for the moratorium and foreclosure scales were negative for the various measures of psychological well-being but non-significant with measures of subjective and eudaimonic well-being.

Liao and Cheng (2011) examined the relationships among emerging adults' identity statuses, self-defining memories and psychological well-being in 114 emerging adult (14 males and 100 females). The findings revealed that identity achievement status positively correlated with all 6 subscales of psychological well-being. Identity diffusion status negatively correlated with all 6 subscales and the composite measure of psychological well-being. Identity moratorium status negatively correlated with 4 of the 6 subscales (autonomy, environmental mastery, purpose of life, and self-acceptance) as well as the composite measure of psychological well-being. Identity foreclosure status negatively correlated with the subscale of purpose of life as well as the composite measure of psychological well-being.

Schwartz, Beyers, Luyckx, et al (2011) studied identity status differences in positive and negative psychosocial functioning. An ethnically diverse sample of 9,034 emerging-adult students (73% female; mean age 19.73 years) from 30 U.S. universities completed measures of identity exploration (ruminative, in breadth, and in depth) and commitment (commitment making and identification with commitment), identity synthesis and confusion, positive and negative psychosocial functioning, and health-compromising behaviors. Findings showed that the two diffused statuses (Carefree-diffusion and diffused diffusion scored lowest on self-esteem, internal locus of control, and all three forms of well-being (satisfaction with life, psychological well-being, and eudaimonic well-being). Both were comparatively high on depression, general anxiety, and social anxiety. Achieved individuals scored highest on all of the positive psychosocial functioning indices. This suggests that high levels of commitment making are associated with feelings of satisfaction and contentment with oneself and with one's life (Rayya, 2006; Luyckx, Schwartz, Goossens & Pollock, 2008; Meeus, Iedema, Helsen & Vollebergh, 1999; Schwartz, 2007).

Sandhu, Singh, Tung and Kundra (2012) aimed to investigate adolescent identityformation in relation to psychological well-being and parental attitudes (viz., acceptance, concentration, and avoidance). For this purpose, a sample of 210 late adolescents (99 boys and 111 girls) with ages ranging from 17 years to 20 years was selected. Findings revealed that for the boys' sample, psychological well-being was positively correlated with identity achievement while opposite pattern emerged for diffusion.

Cakir (2014) examined the role of gender and ego identity status (identity achievement, moratorium, foreclosure, and identity diffusion) in predicting psychological well-being among Turkish emerging adults. The study sample comprised 301 emerging adults aged 19–25 years. Results showed that identity achievement to be a positive predictor of all psychological well-being dimensions whereas moratorium, foreclosure, and identity diffusion were found to be negative predictors of several well-being dimensions. These results suggest that identity commitment following exploration of possible alternatives is an important factor in the psychological well-being of emerging adults in a non-Western cultural context.

Parenting Style

Social support can be defined as supportive relationships with others (DuBois, et al., 2002). Often times these relationships act as resources encouraging favorable adjustment in adolescents. Particularly in adolescents, strong positive interpersonal relationships are beneficial because they function as a source of comfort and safety throughout the multiple life changes that occur during this stage of development (Kenny, Gallagher, Alavarez-Salvat & Silsby, 2002). Two sources of support appear to have the greatest influence on the individual: family and peers. Families stimulate and support the development of distinctive points of view; peers offer models, diversity and opportunities for exploration of beliefs and values (Bosma & Kunnen, 2001). Both play a part during one's development of personal identity. Some studies show that youth are more likely to have difficulty adjusting when sources of social support are not balanced between peer oriented and adult-oriented domains (DuBois, et al., 2002). This argument contends both sources of social support are equally influential. Therefore, it is important to consider both familial and peer influences onthe development of identity.

Parents are viewed as important resources in adolescents' lives. Various authors argue that adolescents' relationships with their parents are significant for their development and general well-being (Markiewicz, Doyle, & Brendgen, 2001). Bradford et al. (2008) indicate that there is an association between parenting and adolescents' well-being across cultures. Adolescents' interaction with their parents is the first social environment with which individuals are confronted. Thus, parents fulfill the role of social agents who convey shared community values and norms to their children and serve as role models with whom they can identify (Koepke & Denissen, 2012).

The previous researches examining the link between parenting and identity have either indirectly assessed a single dimension of parenting, such as attachment (Benson, Harris, & Rogers, 1992; Meeus, Oosterwegel, & Vollebergh, 2002; Schultheiss & Blustein, 1994) or parental separation anxiety (Bartle-Haring, Brucker, & Hock, 2002), or explored the degree of identity achievement rather than the process of identity development (Bhushan & Shirali, 1992; Lucas, 1997). Moreover, investigations conducted with sample sizes comparable to or exceeding the number of participants in this study ($N = 1134$) either combined data for mother and for father and analyzed the parental influence as a unit on identity related outcomes of adolescence (Schmitt-Rodermund & Vondracek, 1999; Steinberg, Lamborn, Dornbusch & Darling, 1992; Steinberg, Mounts, Lamborn & Dornbusch, 1991), or only explored the mother-adolescent relationship (Sartor & Youniss, 2002). While reviewing the literature studies have been found correlating parenting style both with identity status by Marcia and identity style by Berzonsky. Since Berzonsky found strong correlation between identity status and identity style, the studies mentioned below have been divided into two sub-sections accordingly.

Relationship between Parenting Style and Identity Status

Studied about Identity Development from Adolescence to Adulthood Waterman (1982),he observed that, on expanding the identity construct so as to expanded to include the various by which an identity is formed, it is predicted that over time there will be progressive developmental shifts in identity status, that means, from the identity diffusion status into the foreclosure or moratorium status, again the foreclosure into the moratorium status, and from the moratorium into the identity achievement status. Adolescents of authoritative families used most adaptive goal strategies it had expected low levels of failure, task irrelevant behavior and passivity, and the applying self-enhancing attributions. These results explain the basis for knowing some of the processes by which parenting styles influence adolescents' academic success and performance.

Earlier studies found that parents who develop their children with appropriate nurture, independence and firm control, get succeeded in making their children highly competent, socially skilled and proficient. Adolescents who got the experience of authoritarian parentingwith have a greater binding with grades than adolescents who undergo other parenting styles(Dornbusch, Ritter, Leiderman, Roberts & Fraleigh, 1987; Lightfoot, Cole & Cole, 2009).

In a presidential address, Steinberg (1991, 2001) examined the most important ideas to have emerged from the last 25 years of research on adolescent development in the family context and concluded that adolescents benefit the most from having authoritative parents. Moreover, the positive correlation between authoritative parenting and adolescent adjustment appears to transcend ethnicity, socioeconomic status, and family structure. Children's perceptions of mothers' and fathers' parenting behaviors are moderately to highly correlated (Tein, Roosa & Michaels, 1994) and children of divorce do not differ significantly from those from intact families in perceptions of parent behavior (Krakauer, 1992). Ample evidence has been provided in the literature supporting the claim that authoritative parenting transcends many boundaries.

Romano (2004) examined the influence of maternal and paternal parenting behaviors on the identity formation process in late adolescence ($N = 1134$) ranging in age from 18 to 25. The results indicated an association between maternal acceptance and identity achievement. An authoritative parenting style correlated with maternal acceptance and unrelated to firm vs. lax control and psychological autonomy vs. control for both parents. On the other side identity diffusion was significantly correlated with all three dimensions of parenting (parental rejection, lax control, and psychological control).

Cakir & Aydin (2005) in their study of Turkish adolescents found that both authoritative and permissive parenting style were associated with the adolescent identity foreclosure status. No significant links were found between authoritative and democratic parenting styles and other identity status.

Adejuwon (2005) examined the extent to which dimensions of parenting style influence identity formation among the youths in a changing society such as Nigeria. 345 youths (15-24 year olds) were randomly selected. Findings revealed that identity formation is high with low parental demandingness, low autonomy and high parental responsiveness. Identity formation is low, with low parental demandingness, low autonomy and low responsiveness. Furthermore, youths in private schools scored higher on identity formation scale than youths in public schools. Conclusively, parental responsiveness and socioeconomic status were found to be key factors in identity formation of Nigerian youths.

Shuqing, Wenxinand Huichang (2006) studied the development of ego identity and its relations to parenting style and parent-adolescent communication in a sample of 639 middle school students. The results indicated :(1) A progressive developmental trend was found in ego identity statuses from junior to senior high school. In contrast with junior high school students, more second and upper-class students in the senior high school were in the achievement less were in the foreclosure and diffusion. (2)Except that more males were in the achievement than females in the first-class of senior high school, there were no gender differences in the identity statuses of other grades. (3) Indulgent, authoritative and neglectful parenting styles scored higher in the achievement than authoritarian style. Authoritative style has highest scores in the foreclosure. Authoritarian style had highest scores in the diffusion and lowest in the achievement, which showed that it didn't contribute to identity development. (4) Parent-adolescent communication had a positive effect on the achievement and foreclosure, while it had a negative effect on the diffusion.

Studying the effects of parenting styles on Identity formation and extent of adjustment among college students, Luyckx, Soenens, Goossens and Vansteenkiste (2007) observed that parents who apply authoritative parenting styles realize that they are responsible for all behaviors of their children and they get assured that their children develop a type of independence. These parents encourage and motivate their children in always all aspects of life and as a result of which their children, when they grow to become adolescents included better personal identity as compared to other children who experience demanding parenting styles in the family. In agreement to this Wargo (2007) in Adolescents and Risk: Helping Young People Make Better Choices demonstrated that an authoritative parenting style produces a number of positive developments in adolescents. Authoritative parenting style which includes parental monitoring and supervision encourages teen's exposure to positive actions and lowers his opportunities for getting engaged in delinquent, risky behaviors.

Khalatbari, Maddahi and Ghorbanshiroudi (2011) aimed to explore the relationship between child rearing styles and identity statuses. A sample of 150 female and male students of Rasht's pre-university level was selected. There existed a significant negative relationship between parent authoritative style and diffused. Findings showed significant positive relationship between diffusion and parent authoritarian style. Advanced or achieved identity found to be significantly related with authoritative style and thereby play an effective role in development of well-defined identity.

Lam and Tam (2011) to identified the correlates of identity statuses among 1260 secondary 2-4 (equivalent to Grades 8–10 in the US school system) Chinese adolescents. They studied the identity statuses with (i) parental and school contexts and (ii) major psychosocial developmental outcomes. Results indicated that parental attributes of acceptance, values and goals, and psychological control, and school contextual factor of task orientations predicted identity achievement, whereas parents' acceptance, psychological and firm control, and teacher's support predicted identity foreclosure. Findings also revealed that (i) identity achievement predicted low depression, high self-esteem, and high self-efficacy; (ii) moratorium predicted low self-esteem; and (iii) foreclosure predicted high self-efficacy.

McKendrick (2011) investigated whether emerging adults' gender differentially influences the perceptions of mother (figure's) parenting style and subsequently identity formation in 124 African American undergraduates. Results revealed no significant differences in perceptions of mother (figures') parenting style based on gender. However, there were other specific differences noted. Emerging adults in this sample who perceived of their mother (figures) as authoritative were more likely undifferentiated in identity status; females in this status were more likely than males to perceive of their parenting as authoritarian. The findings of this study appear to have implications for developing parent education in African American families and interventions for young adults who may be experiencing identity confusion.

Bleistein (2012) explored the relationship between parenting styles and identity status in a sample of 122 undergraduates (99 females, 23 males). The highest parenting style scores were for authoritativeness, followed by permissiveness, authoritarianism, and neglect. The highest identity status scores were for achievement, followed by moratorium, diffusion, and foreclosure. The correlational analyses focused on sons and daughters separately. Mother authoritativeness was not associated with any identity status variable. As expected, higher scores for father authoritativeness were associated with higher levels of identity achievement, but only for daughters, and with higher levels of moratorium, but only for sons. Unexpectedly, higher levels of identity achievement in sons were associated with father authoritarianism; authoritarianism was not significantly associated with foreclosure in either sons or daughters. Also contrary to expectations, higher levels of permissiveness were not related to identity diffusion; instead, they tended to be associated with foreclosure in daughters and with moratorium in sons. As expected, parent neglect was positively associated with identity diffusion at trend levels, but only for sons. Some of the unexpected results may be explained by gender role differences in autonomy and relationality. Sons may move toward identity achievement as a strategy to obtain independence from rigid fathers. Likewise, daughters may foreclose in order to provide missing structure in their relationships with permissive parents.

Esmaeili, Farrokhi, Nikakhlagh & Yousefi (2014) investigated the role of parenting styles and religious adherence on the identity of high school students in Iran. For the purpose, 500 high school students (250 boys and 250 girls) were selected by cluster random sampling. The results showed that the authoritarian parenting style suspension identity in boys and girls, religious adherence suspension in girls' identity, religious adherence foreclosure democratic parenting style, permissive parenting style and religious adherence identity religious adherence identity crisis in boys and girls and the boys realized that there is a significant relationship. The results suggested that in addition to parenting styles and religious adherence, other factors may also shape - the effective identity of the peer, mental health training received socioeconomic status, personality and mutual influence of parent teenager on each other.

Ahadi, Hejazi & Foumany (2014) studied the relationship between parenting styles and adolescent's identity and aggression. Adolescents (100 male and 100 female) aged 14 to 18 along with their parents were selected. Their results indicated that the relationship between parenting style and aggression is not significant. With regard to the relationship between parenting style and identity formation, authoritative (democratic) parenting has relationship with the formation of premature identity subscale, diffusion and advanced. Authoritarian style has relationship with all identity subscales and permissive style has relationship with the formation of identity diffusion, premature identity.

Grové & Naudé (2015) aimed to investigate the relationship between ego identity statuses and perceived parenting styles in black adolescents living in different family structures. A sample of 188 participants was selected from four high schools in the Mangaung area. The majority of black adolescents in the sample did not live with their biological parents and reported living in a non-nuclear family. No statistically significant differences were reported between ego identity statuses and perceived parenting styles in nuclear and non-nuclear family structures. Finally, significant positive correlations were found between a diffused status and an authoritative parenting style, as well as between an achieved status and a permissive parenting style. It has been concluded that the permissive parenting style promotes development of ego identity (achieved status) and that the authoritative parenting style restricts development of ego identity (diffused status) among black adolescents living in the Mangaung area. Differences in the interpretation of a mature ego identity status between individualistic and collectivistic practices (Cheng & Berman, 2012; Smits et al., 2008; Steinberg, 2000), have been identified as a possible clarification for the results. It can be argued that adolescents and black families living in South Africa today are constantly facing social challenges because of the changing social context in South Africa. This situation might affect the identity development, parenting styles, and family structures in which they live.

Laboviti (2015) studied the relations between the parenting styles and identity status of teenagers in Albanian context in a sample of participants (N=129) where 65 were parents and 64 teenagers of age 14-18. The results showed a moderated relation between the liberal (permissive) parenting style and the diffused status of identity, but did not show a relation between the authoritarian parenting style and imposed (foreclosed) status of identity and did not show any relation between the authoritarian style and the matured status or moratorium at all.

Alfonso, Sun & Schalkwyk (2015) examined the role of perceived parenting styles in the choice of identity processing and commitment among a group of 209 Chinese youth. The findings showed a positive relation between authoritative parenting and informational processing and identity commitment. However, a negative relation between a normative processing style and identity commitment was found in the Chinese sample. Youth from authoritative families were more likely to use the information processing style, perceiving their parents as more responsive to their needs and forthcoming with information necessary for identity commitment. The youth from authoritarian families adopted a normative processing style, perceiving their parents as less responsiveness and possibly more demanding of conformity to existing norms in society. Individuals perceiving their parents as permissive were more inclined towards a diffuse-avoidant social cognitive identity processing style, given that their parents were purportedly less demanding although moderately communicative. Furthermore, the strong positive correlation between authoritative and permissive parenting styles needs further exploration and questioning of the parenting typology commonly used in Western countries. Chinese youth apparently do not perceive their parents as 'permissive' when the parents pose fewer demands and controls on their socio-cognitive explorations, focusing rather on the parents' responsiveness to their needs. On the other hand, the demandingness embedded within the authoritative parenting style is perceived as benevolent control and supportive of socio-cognitive explorations (Chen, Dong & Zhou, 1997; Lee, Pratto & Li, 2007).

Aveh and Jalalat (2015) identified the role of parental styles and emotional autonomy in establishing identity styles and identity. A sample of 237 Iranian male and female students of age group 15-17 years was drawn. Results indicated that positive identity was positively correlated with authoritative parental style and emotional autonomy and negatively with authoritarian. The results indicated that emotional autonomy and parental styles variables combined accounted for 46% of the variation in strength of positive identity.

Rageliene and Justickis (2016) aimed to strengthen the understanding of the pathways through which parenting style shapes adolescent's identity development by addressing two aims. First, it considered whether parenting style is related to adolescent's identity development. Second, it examined whether differentiation of self-mediate the links between parenting style and identity development. 804 adolescents were selected for the purpose. Adolescent differentiation of self fully mediates the relationship between authoritarian and democratic parenting style and identity diffusion in the sample of boys. The democratic parenting style positively predicts differentiation of self for boys, while authoritarian parenting style negatively predicts this relationship for both genders. In this case, differentiation of self negatively predicts the identity diffusion of adolescents of both genders. In the sample of girls, differentiation of self only partially mediates the relation between authoritarian parenting style and identity diffusion. Results of this study have also shown that permissive parenting style does not predict identity diffusion for boys, but, positively predicts identity diffusion in girls' sample. Because identity diffusion is considered to be related with adolescents' mental health problems (Dumas et al., 2009; Jung et al., 2013; Ramgoon et al., 2006) positive links between the girls' identity diffusion and permissive parenting style could be explained considering the results of other researches. According to Renen & Wild (2008) lower levels of connection and regulation from parents (this is characteristics of permissive parenting style) are related with more reported suicidal ideation or behavior by adolescents. Poor parent-child relationship, low parental interest and monitoring are related with a greater risk of adolescent reporting abnormal levels of emotional and behavior problems (Giannakopoulos et al., 2009). Permissive parenting is also positively related with the conduct disorder (Smith & Hall, 2008). Permissive parenting style includes more lax, inconsistent, and avoidant behaviors (Baumrind, 1966).

Aldhafri & Al-Harthy (2016) examined the relationship between university students' academic identity and their perceptions of their parents' parenting styles among a sample of Omani students. The findings show that parenting styles varied in their relationship with the four statuses of students' academic identity. Parenting styles correlated significantly with moratorium levels, three of the styles correlated positively with diffusion, with the exception being authoritative style, which correlated negatively. When examined in relation to achievement, authoritative style correlated positively while permissive style correlated negatively. Authoritarian parenting style correlation with achievement was not significant.

Rezvani, Gowda and D'Souza (2017) assessed the relation between parenting styles and identity formation status of adolescents studying in a sample of 400 adolescents (200 early and 200 late adolescents) of Mysore city. Results revealed that, adolescents with authoritarian parenting styles had higher personal identity formation than adolescents with permissive and authoritarian parenting styles. Developmental stage showed significant influence on all components of identity-Personal, Relational, Social and Collective, where in early stage adolescents had higher identity than adolescents at later stage.

Relationship between Parenting Style and Identity Style

Berzonsky (2004) studied the relationship between identity style, parental authority, and identity commitment. Adolescents with an information-oriented identity style were found to perceive their parents as authoritative and as engaging in open communication (Berzonsky, Branje & Meeus, in press). In line with expectations, he found a normative identity style to relate to perceptions of authoritarian parenting. Adams, Berzonsky and Keating (2006) found that these adolescents perceive their family as lacking expressiveness (i.e., lack of openness to ideas and feelings). Unexpectedly, a normative style also related positively to authoritativeness and cohesive, trusting family relations (Adams et al., 2006; Berzonsky et al., in press). Finally, a diffuse avoidant style was found to relate to authoritarianism and permissiveness (Berzonsky, 2004) and lack of expressiveness in family communications (Adams et al., 2006).

Smits et al. (2008) in a sample of middle and late adolescents (n = 674) examined the relationships between crucial dimensions of perceived parenting (support, behavioral control, and psychological control) and the three identity styles defined by Berzonsky. Their findings revealed that an information-oriented style was positively predicted by parental support. Contrary to expectations, however, an information-oriented style was also positively predicted by psychological control. A normative identity style was positively predicted by support and behavioral control. In line with expectations, a diffuse-avoidant identity style was positively predicted by psychological control and negatively by maternal (but not paternal) behavioral control.

Çelen & Kuşdil (2009) explored the relationships between identity styles and perceived parenting control patterns in late adolescents of their 402 Turkish university students. Findings revealed that adolescents who live with authoritarian parents also acquire informational identity style. This kind of parenting style has been considered as "pathological" by Western psychologists, but others argue that this may not be the case in Eastern cultures (Kagitcibasi, 1996). Psychological outcomes of authoritarian parenting styles are not same in all contexts. Authoritative parenting style predicted four identity styles in an expected way. Higher levels of authoritative style are related to higher scores for commitment and informational identity styles and lower levels of authoritative style are related to higher scores for norm-oriented and diffuse/avoidant identity styles. Several identity studies (LaVoie, 1976; Josselson, 1987) argue that different socialization processes (i.e. parents' child-rearing style) may lead to different identity styles and statuses.

Ratner (2013) investigated the possibility of attachment playing a mediational role in the relationship between parenting and identity style. A total of 264 students from two high schools participated in this study. It was found that only maternal parenting style was related to identity style, and it was only significant for the informational and normative identity styles. This finding could have been due to a number of reasons, but the most practical explanation could lie in the fact that many more students reported having some kind of maternal figure than a paternal figure. Parenting style was not found to have a significant impact on the diffuse-avoidant identity style in any case. The parenting style dimensions assessed during this study, responsiveness and demandingness, were shown to have various significant relationships with each of the identity styles regardless of parental gender It was found that authoritative mothers elicited significantly more informational adolescents than negligent or authoritarian mothers, but not indulgent mothers. Interestingly, indulgent mothers fostered the informational identity style more so than negligent or authoritarian mothers, just as authoritative mothers. However, no significant difference was observed between the indulgent and authoritative parenting style in terms of informational development.

An attempt was made by Abaspoorazar, Farrokhi and Ali (2015) to explain the relationship between parenting styles, identity styles and spiritual health in adolescents. 628 high school students (311 females and 317 males) were selected for the study. The results showed that the identity, informational and normative styles have significant and positive relation with spiritual health and have no significant relationship with avoiding or diffused identity. Authoritative style of parenting practices has a significant and positive correlation with the spiritual health and authoritarian style has a significant and negative relation with spiritual health. The results obtained on the relation between parenting practices and identity styles indicate that authoritative parenting practices has a positive relation with normative identity and negative relationship with avoidant identity. Also, authoritarian parenting style has a negative relation with informational and normative identity and significant and positive correlation with avoidant identity and only easy-going parenting style has a significant and negative correlation with informational identity.

Far & Fattahi (2015) conducted a study to investigate relationship between parenting styles and identity styles. The findings revealed a significant correlation between some of components of parenting styles and identity styles. There was a significant positive correlation between authoritative parenting style and informative identity. Parents who have authoritative parenting style their adolescent children have more identity progress and have more commitment identity, informative and normative identity. Results showed that among authoritative, authoritarian and permissive parenting style, authoritative style has significant negative correlation with confusion identity and authoritarian and permissive has significant positive correlation with confusion. It means that parents, who train their children by coercive, authoritarian methods and also do not respond to their emotional and mental health needs of, likely can have important role in adolescents' confusion identity formation. These parents use less method of interaction with restriction of freedom and observance of discipline that is characteristic of authoritarian parenting style. Authoritarian and permissive style can be important factor in undesirable and confusing identity formation. Their results were also consistent with findings of Samuolis *et al.* (2001) which in their study concluded that attachment to both parents has positive relationship with identity commitment and also results in consistent of Frank *et al.* (1990) study that showed disoriented relationship between parents – adolescent positive relationship with distributed identity and negatively correlated with development of identity. Adolescent identity commitment is mostly caused by emotional relationships with parents. Research of Adams (1992) indicated that anonymous teenagers often been forgotten or were rejected by their parents, perhaps reason is that when replication is done with their characteristics that adolescents have attachment to them.

With regards to the results of discussed studies, two major issues unveiled. First, contradictions exist between the links of relationship of parenting style and adolescents' identity development. It could be explained by various external and internal factors, such as family socioeconomic status, age, ethnicity or gender of adolescents and their parents, or character traits, lifestyle, communication skills, emotionality or other personality related factors that may mediate relationship between parenting style and adolescents' identity development. To conclude, there is a lack of studies investigating the explicit relationships between parenting styles and adolescents' identity development. Second, contradictory results in this area also highlight the importance of new empirical research in this area, especially in Indian or Eastern context. Most of the previous studies have been carried out in Western contexts which appeared to differ from individualistic to collectivist. Thus it enabled the researcher to shed light on the explicit role of parenting style in the development of diffused identity in Indian context.

Attribution Style

While reviewing, research on the relationship between attribution style and identity statuses has been noticeably missing from the extant literature. A plethora of findings revealed the association between locus of control and identity status or optimism and identity status. It enabled the researcher to select the variable in present study by considering the following findings.

Research on a possible link between identity and locus of control grew from investigations that showed youth became more internal in their locus of control as they matured (Matteson, 1977). Several researchers also found that the external locus of control position declines over the course of adolescence (Cairns, McWhirter, Duffy & Barry, 1990; Chubb, Fertman & Ross, 1997; Knoop, 1981). Longitudinal studies of identity development have shown movement from Marcia's (1966) foreclosure and diffusion identity status positions to the moratorium and achievement positions over adolescence and early adulthood (e.g., Kroger, Martinussen & Marcia, 2010). Somewhat mixed results have appeared when investigators have examined the relationship between locus of control and identity status over the past three decades.

Waterman, Buebel and Waterman (1970) were the first investigators to examine the relationship between locus of control and Marcia's (1966) identity statuses. Their investigation divided the identity statuses into high (achievement and moratorium), mixed, and low (foreclosure and diffusion) groups. Those in the high identity status group showed a more internal locus of control on Rotter's Internal-External (I-E) scale than those in the low identity status group. The findings are in agreement to other earlier researches (Howard, 1975; Adams and Shea, 1979, Francis, 1981) revealing committed statuses had a higher tendency toward the internal locus of control position than statuses that were not committed.

On the other side, Matteson (1977) obtained different result while examining the relationship between 12 personality variables, including locus of control, in relation to the dimensions of exploration and commitment as well as identity status. He selected a sample of 99 Danish youth and found no significant relationship with identity status. Similarly different result was obtained in a study done by Ginsburg & Orlofsky (1981) investigating the relationship of identity status to ego development and locus of control in 75 college women. The identity statuses did not differ significantly in self-reported locus of control, but did differ on the "depth" measure of ego development. Consistent with identity theory and with previous research with males, identity achievers and moratorium (in crisis) women were more advanced in their ego development than fore-closure and diffusion women.

Abraham (1983) studied the relationship between locus of control and identity status in a sample of 223 high school students from 9th-12th graders. Results confirmed that identity achievement individuals were significantly less external in locus of control than individuals in all other identity statuses and diffused were significantly more external in locus of control. Some studies have shown that the moratorium status has a higher internal locus of control than the foreclosure and diffusion statuses. McConnell (1986) explained this finding by arguing that moratoriums are in the process of forming and internalizing values which, in turn, results in the higher locus of control score. Other studies have found moratoriums to have a more external locus of control (Evans & Bloom, 1996).

Mozaffari, Jalil & Bagherian (2009) explored the interrelations between identity status and locus of control with gender, grade and field among high school students (179 male and 167 female students). Findings revealed no significant difference between boys and girls in their identity status. The findings showed senior students were more successful in accessing achieving identity status than junior students.

Results also showed a meaningful relationship between locus of control and gender. Cording to the findings, female students and students studding humanities showed more external locus of control than others. On the other hand, male students and students majoring in mathematics showed more internal locos of control. In addition, the results revealed a significant relationship between identity status and locus of control: those with achieved identity status had more internal locus of control than diffused.

Lillevoll, Kroger & Martinussen (2013) conducted a meta-analysis to examine the relationship between identity status and locus of control through techniques of meta-analysis. A total of 565 empirical studies of identity status that were conducted between 1966 and 2005 were identified from Psych INFO, ERIC, Sociological Abstracts, and Dissertation Abstracts International using these search terms: "identity status," "identity and Marcia," "identity and Marcia's," and "ego identity." Nineteen of these studies addressed the relationship between locus of control and identity status; only five of the studies ($N \frac{1}{4} 711$ participants) provided data with satisfactory information to be included in the meta-analysis. Internal and external locus of control scales were correlated with each identity status. Identity diffusion found to be negatively correlated with internal locus of control and moderately positively with external locus of control.

Janarthanam and Gnanadevan (2015) studied the relationship between identity statuses and locus of control of higher secondary students. The samples of the study were 800 adolescents' students (410 boys and 390 girls) studying higher secondary in Cuddalore District of Tamil Nadu, India. The findings indicated that the locus of control is negatively correlated with identity diffusion. It further indicates that the locus of control is positively correlated with identity foreclosure and identity achievement. There is no significant correlation found between locus of control and identity moratorium.

Within attribution style is embedded locus of control. However, the locus of control is concerned with expectancies about the future while attribution style is concerned with attributions for the past. Whereas locus of control cuts across both positive and negative outcomes, authors in the attribution style field have distinguished between a Pessimistic Explanatory Style, in which failures are attributed to internal, stable, and global factors and successes to external, unstable, and specific causes, and an Optimistic Explanatory Style, in which successes are attributed to internal, stable, and global factors and failures to external, unstable, and specific causes.

Decision Making Styles

The placement of a person into one of four identity statuses depends upon the process by which that person establishes, or fails to establish, certain occupational and ideological commitments. This fact suggests that the decision process, or cognitive style, used by a person in establishing an identity status could be indicative of a more general decision style. That is, the identity statuses can be seen as "individual styles of coping with the psychosocial task of forming an ego identity" (Marcia, 1966). If this were the case, it might be possible to predict successful resolution of the identity crisis by assessing cognitive style prior to adolescence.

Many researchers have stated that decision making skills should be taught routinely during adolescence, at an age when vital choices are already being made (Baron, 1989; Mann, Harmoni & Power, 1989; Hardin & Leong, 2004).

Blustein and Philips (1990) examined the proposition that individual variations in career decision making are related conceptually to the identity formation process of late adolescence. To investigate this proposition 2 studies were conducted to identify the relations between ego identity statuses and decision-making styles. The findings suggested that persons who have achieved a stable identity tend to use rational and systematic decision-making strategies. Those whose identity status is foreclosed tend to rely on dependent strategies and do not endorse systematic and internal strategies. Persons in the diffusion status tend to rely on intuitive and dependent styles or exhibit an absence of systematic and internal styles. The moratorium status was not consistently associated with variations in decision-making styles. Their results indicated that identity versus identity diffusion psychosocial-developmental task is related to career decision-making styles.

Kuzgun (2005) identified four different general decision-making styles: rational, intuitive, dependent, and indecisiveness. The rational style is characterized by systematic and planful strategies with a clear future orientation. The rational decision-makers accept responsibility for choice that is derived from an internal locus of control and are active, deliberate and logical. Identity-achieved persons have gone through a period of exploration and have made a commitment to a specific decision after careful exploration. These persons typically use planful strategies (e.g., rational style). The intuitive style is characterized by the reliance on inner experience, fantasy, and a propensity to decide rapidly without much deliberation or information gathering. The intuitive decision makers accept responsibility for choice, but focus on emotional self- awareness, fantasy and feeling, often in impulsive manner (Harren,

1979; Rubinton, 1980; Kuzgun, 1995; Payne et al., 1993). Persons in the moratorium status are currently in the process of exploration and commitments are either vague or absent rely on this style. Identity diffused persons may have undergone some explorations, but they seem to be meandering more than actively exploring. The overriding decisional characteristic of the diffusion status is the tendency to avoid decision- making situations .These persons may rely on intuitive and spontaneous styles or may seek answers from others (as in the dependent style and the indecisiveness style) to reduce the deliberation and consequent anxiety (Marcia, 1980). The dependent decision- making style involves denying responsibility for their choices and projects responsibility towards others, generally authority figures. The persons in the foreclosure status generally tend to depend on others (e.g., friends, family, and authority figures) in resolving decisions related to identity concerns and likely to seek out rapid, non-deliberate solutions to decision- making tasks (Marcia, 1980; A. S. Waterman, 1985). These persons are not likely to use systematic or rational approaches that are also derived from an external locus of responsibility (Cella et al., 1987; Marcia, 1980).

Bacanli (2012) examined the nature of the relations amongst four general decision making styles and ego identity statuses. 298 Turkish freshmen university students (168 female and 130 male)were selected. The results indicated that identity-achievement status was positively related to rational decision- making style, but it was negatively related to dependent and indecisiveness styles. Diffusion, foreclosure and moratorium statuses were positively related to the intuitive and indecisiveness styles.

Pellerone (2013) investigated the relation between identity status, coping style and general decision making styles among group of 82 Italian university students. The result showed a significant correlation between high profile/well defined identity and rational style. Low profile or diffused identity tends to use avoidance coping strategies and avoidant decision style. They tend to score lower on academic success and self-exploration.

Studies on Identity Interventions

In the mid-1980s, Marcia (1986) first described the possible implications that the identity status paradigm held for intervention in educational and clinical settings. He warned against requiring occupational or other major educational decisions in early adolescence, and he made a plea that professional degree programs should provide opportunities for the study and exploration of ideas and values rather than accelerated degree acquisition. Marcia also discussed forms of clinical intervention likely to be effective with individuals in each identity status.

Archer (1994) produced the first edited volume that considered the implications of identity and identity status interventions across a wide range of contexts—from psychotherapy to the family, and from ethnic minority adolescents to educational settings. Contributors to that volume reflected on a range of issues essential to intervention programs encouraging identity exploration and self-discovery. However, research on the actual applications of identity and identity status interventions has begun only more recently.

Short term intervention for identity development

One of the first systematic attempts to assess results of an intervention program aimed to facilitate identity status development in late adolescence was undertaken by

Markstrom-Adams, Ascione, Braegger and Adams (1993). These researchers introduced a short-term perspective training program aimed particularly at increasing identity exploration. However, their two studies ailed to show significant results, and the authors concluded that it was difficult to promote substantial identity development through short-term intervention programs. These results have been largely re-echoed through various doctoral studies that have attempted to implement short-term strategies to facilitate identity status change (e.g., Edward, 1981; Hall, 1994; Wentz, 1986).

More recently, intervention attempts have targeted areas such as knowledge, attitudes, and exploration/commitment dimensions of identity in marginalized youth. Ferrer-Wreder et al. (2002) examined the impact of a one-semester intervention program for marginalized youth on the specific developmental domains of skills/knowledge, attitudes, orientations, and exploration/commitment dimensions linked to identity. Although immediate intervention gains were apparent, these gains were not well maintained over time. From these studies, it seems that identity exploration and consolidation requires time and readiness for development to proceed, and short-term intervention efforts(e.g., sessions over the course of several weeks or months) have, in general, not been particularly effective in facilitating long-term identity development.

Intervention based on Promoting Positive identity

An individual's identity profile (strengths and weaknesses across the different identity domains), identity status (including the interplay of exploration and commitment, the magnitude of discrepancies between real and ideal self), and the ability of that individual to effect necessary improvement to his or her identity development, all have an impact on the immediate positive and negative aspects of the individual's well-being. In addition, it will affect one's long-term development into adulthood and the future stages of one's life span. Positive indicators include self-esteem, life satisfaction, positive effect, quality of life, environmental mastery, positive relations with others like parents (Berzonsky, Branje and Meeus, 2007), teachers, and peers, and self-acceptance. Negative indicators include internalizing pathology like stress, depression, and anxiety, as well as externalizing pathological behavior like hostility, aggression, loss of control, and disruptive behavior (Sharma and Sharma, 2010; Jensen, 2011). Many such indicators are included as positive youth development constructs in Project PATHS, a positive youth development program developed and validated for Chinese adolescents. The enhancement of positive identity development in young people can be achieved at both the individual and the social levels.

Catalano (2004), a researcher on positive youth development programs, conceptualized positive youth identity as "the internal organization of a coherent sense of self". He found that "positive identity" was treated as a core construct in nine out of 25 effective positive youth development programs. Specific strategies adopted by these programs to enhance positive identity include the following.

Promoting Self-Esteem

According to Harter (1999) one's evaluation of oneself, often called self-esteem, can influence identity formation and the emotions and performance related to it. Positive self-evaluation typically energizes a person while negative self-evaluation, especially when it is prolonged and hinges upon attributes that cannot be easily changed or acquired, can disturb person's emotions and performance.

Borba's Esteem Builders curriculum is one of the most comprehensive and widely used skills-based curricula (1999). Its theoretical framework is inspired by Branden (1994) who defined self-esteem as "the disposition to experience oneself as competent to cope with the basic challenges of life and as worthy of happiness." Borba emphasized five acquired components of authentic self-esteem: (a) security, the feeling of strong assuredness; (b) selfhood, the feeling of self-worth and accurate identity; (c) affiliation, the feeling of belonging and social acceptance; (d) mission, the feeling of purpose; and (e) competence, the feeling of self-empowerment and efficacy. In Hong Kong, the Tung Wah Group of Hospitals indigenized Borba's Esteem Builder curriculum in 1993 and developed programs for use in schools from preschools to secondary schools. The Project PATHS developed to enhance positive youth development also built on Borba's model by working on the key components of self-esteem enhancement and identity exploration. The aim is to enhance junior secondary school students' skills in recognizing their self-image, reducing self-discrepancies, and increasing positive self-talk. The curriculum will also use societal expectations of appropriate gender roles and identity to sharpen gender-sensitive discussions. Skills taught include positive self-evaluation, assertiveness affirmation skills, and understanding and dealing with social expectations and undue negative comments.

Reducing Self-Discrepancies

During the process of identity search, adolescents often encounter discrepancies between their ideal self, real self, self-perceived self, and their self as perceived by others, or discrepancies between personal and social identities. Such discrepancies will expose adolescents to increased psychosocial risks like emotional and behavioral problems. By identifying the nature and magnitude of such discrepancies, steps can be taken to reduce these disturbing discrepancies, reinforce identity clarity and commitment, and even promote self-esteem (Higgins, 1987; Meeus, 2002).

Aside from working directly on the individuals themselves, effective management of risk and protective contextual determinants is also important for fostering positive identity. Traditionally, schools and families are the two most influential developmental contexts for adolescents who normally live at home and study in schools. The physical and psychosocial environments at home and school, the resources of those entities, the opportunities they provide, the support and recognition they give to the youths, together with their rules and values all influence the identity development of the youths. Schools and families exist in specific cultural and subcultural contexts, and the characteristics of such, like gender role expectations, religiosity, and achievement expectations, also release positive or negative energies that influence identity development. In recent decades, penetration of adolescents' daily lives by the media and the internet has enabled young people to access local and global, as well as factual and virtual contexts. In urbanized cities like Hong Kong, young people can command greater information technology than their parents and even their teachers, making it very difficult for adults to provide appropriate guidance to the young (Valkenburgh and Peter, 2008). The virtual environment enables the manipulation of made-up identities for explorative social interactions. How to keep such "exploration" within functional and adaptive limits is certainly a challenge to information-technology-driven modern life styles. An effective use of such channels should be able to prepare adolescents better to go through their adolescence and be best prepared for adulthood.

A small-scale exploratory evaluation of the Exploration Enhancement Workshop, a university-based intervention for enhancing identity exploration among emerging adults was conducted by Schwartz et al. (2005). The sample for the study included 90 students at a public university. For its intervention strategy, the program used a group-based empowerment approach which drew on Freire's (1970-1983) transformative pedagogy to help participants identify life challenges and work together to co-construct solutions to these challenges. The intervention team participated as co-learners in dialogue with the students rather than as experts transferring knowledge to students. Although the study was exploratory and limited by its scale, Schwartz and colleagues (2005) found cognitive intervention strategies were effective in promoting self-construction, while emotion-focused strategies were effective in promoting self-discovery identity processes. These findings suggested that both cognitive and emotion-focused strategies should be included in identity-focused interventions for emerging adults (Schwartz et al., 2005).

Daytona Adult Identity Development Program (Berman et al., 2008) like the exploration enhancement workshop used a participatory transformative approach to expand self-understanding and insight through identity exploration, teach critical thinking and problem solving skills, and adaptive functioning and the ability to integrate aspects of the self into a relatively coherent and acceptable sense of self (Erikson, 1950; Luyckx et al., 2008; Montgomery, Hernandez & Ferrer-Wreder, 2008a). Berman and colleagues (2004) found that, in a nonclinical sample of 331 university students, 12% experienced identity-related distress, meeting the DSM-III-Rcriteria for identity disorder (American Psychiatric Association, 1987). Although experiencing a certain amount of distress is normative and a key component of the identity process, prolonged or severe identity distress can lead young people to adhere to a negative identity (i.e., adherence to an identity that involves high psychological and physical risk for the individual) or a diffused sense of self (Montgomery, Hernandez & Ferrer-Wreder, 2008).

Intervention based on Psychotherapy

Folesch, Odom and Kernberg (2008) examined a treatment modified from a therapy that has been found to be effective in the treatment of adults with significant identity diffusion, namely, Transference Focused Psychotherapy. The central role of differentiating normal Identity Crisis from Identity Diffusion in adolescents, essential to accurately identifying those adolescents appropriate for this treatment, is articulated. The primary modifications of TFP for adolescent treatment described involve changes in frequency and duration of some of the specific techniques (e.g. increased clarification ; more work in the extra-transferential relationships before directly addressing the transference), tactics (e.g. inclusion of family during the assessment phase and treatment contract setting phases of treatment; inclusion of supportive interventions in the environment while maintaining the analytic stance in sessions), and strategies (e.g. the goal of removing blockages to the development of normal identity integration, not "forced maturation"). This treatment aims to improve adolescent's relationships with friends, parents, and teachers; help clarify life goals; acquire positive self-esteem; and be better prepared for entering love relationships.

Intervention based on Music therapy

The emergence of music therapy in schools has allowed vulnerable youth to confront these developmental issues through music. Music therapists have traditionally practiced with populations with special needs, such as those with developmental disabilities or dementia, but during the past two decades they have also worked more frequently with youth at risk (Duerksen & Darrow, 1991). Music therapy is a process used to restore, improve, or maintain wellbeing; however, it becomes educational when the participants gain skills or content found in the music curriculum (Bruscia, 1989).

Derrington (2005), a British music therapist working in a mainstream school, showed that songwriting allows youth to discuss difficult issues, since lyrics can be less direct than conversation, and that group songwriting can increase confidence and independence, changing negative interactions into positive ones through a shared process involving listening and supporting.

Austin (2007), an American music therapist helping inner city youth, has used rap as a means of personal disclosure and affirmation. She observed that identity in adolescence is mutable and that these young people often have difficulty with identity formation since they have not completed the earlier stages of development and their basic needs have not been met; this would identify them as diffused. She realized that music can serve as a constant, unlike the familial relationships these youth have experienced, and favorite songs can be played as needed for comfort and security. Austin found that adolescents' preferred songs often mirror hidden thoughts and feelings, which can be discussed and made clear, while identification with a singer can help strengthen a sense of self and foster peer relationships. The use of popular music can help adolescents' — increase self-awareness, build self-esteem, strengthen their identities and solidify their connection to others (Austin, 2007).

Buchanan (2000), a music therapist working in a Canadian alternative school, found that active music-making is a means to allow youth an appropriate method of venting frustration and anger. She also noted that group music activities foster relationships and respect for others, and that disclosure and self-awareness occur as relationships develop. This indicates identity achievement is occurring.

Intervention based on psychosocial education

Navyashree (2015) studied the effect of psychosocial education on adolescents in order to improve the identity, achievement motivation, need for intimacy and autonomy among adolescents. For the purpose of the study 81 adolescents comprising of boys and girls of age range 15 to 16 years was selected. Intervention consisted of training programs on communication skills development, stress management, effective decision making, problem solving skills, responsible use of autonomy, importance of maintaining healthy positive relationships, career choices and selection, positive identity development, goal setting and achievement. Obtained results showed that there is a significant effect of psychosocial education on adolescents' achievement motivation, autonomy and identity. Achievement motivation, personal identity, social identity, cultural identity, need for autonomy was significantly higher post intervention.

Common to intervention theory and research to date is the suggestion that differential intervention strategies must to be targeted to individuals in each of the distinct identity statuses.

Based on the research findings, the present study aims at investigating the role of resilience, well-being, parenting style, attribution style and decision making style in determining identity diffusion status in adolescents.

CHAPTER 3

METHODOLOGY

METHODOLOGY

RATIONALE OF THE STUDY

"Adolescence" an age of turmoil and tribulations, a developmental transition period between childhood and adulthood often signals a restructuring of the self. It is the developmental stage when the crisis to resolve the conflict of identity confusion vs. identity formation is prioritized (Erikson, 1968). This stage marks the formation of identity status among adolescents that is often termed as ego identity status. An established ego identity is a foundation for effective functioning of the adolescent's personality characterized by exploration and commitment (Lubenko & Sebre, 2007). Therefore, it is important to understand the development of adolescents' ego identity and the factors that affect it positively or negatively (Geldard and Geldard, 2010). Marcia (1966) indicates that adolescents' ego identity status is based on their exploration and commitment. He identifies four categories of ego identity status, namely identity achievement, diffusion, moratorium, and foreclosure. Of the four identity statuses, identity diffusion is considered to be the most impaired status which needs further investigation.

A person with a diffused identity status is not able to define his or her personal strength and weaknesses and does not have a well articulate sense of self. They neither explore the options nor commit to decisions. They lack academically, socially and have poor interpersonal relations (Campbell, Adams & Dobson, 1984; Josselson, 1987; Orlofsky, Marcia & Lesser, 1973). Since they are adolescents and have a whole life ahead to shape themselves so it is utmost important to know the factors responsible for diffusion. Development of ego identity is influenced by personal and social factors (Erikson, 1968). Carter and McGoldrick (1989) argue that adolescence is a challenging time for a family because parent-adolescent conflict increases when adolescents start searching for autonomy. Therefore, an investigation into the current parenting styles and their role in the development of identity which is either achieved or diffused can yield valuable information. Contemporary researches also emphasized the role of various personality and cognitive variables in the development of one's identity (Grotevant, 1987; Cramer, 2000). If the adolescence is spent without considerable difficulty, the adolescent will change into a healthy adult person with clear defined identity. If they fail in resolving their crisis it will lead diffused identity. A diffused individual has a negative approach to life, low resilience, poor cognitive functioning thereby resulting into poor well-being. While reviewing the literature, no direct association between identity status and attribution style was obtained. Studies showed the links between stress, coping and identity but did not show its association with resilience. Therefore, it could be argued that development of ego identity is still a relevant concept today because of the complexity of the construct *ego identity*. However, most of the studies were conducted in western settings, and Indian studies are limited. In addition, development of ego identity differs between different culture and ethnic groups. Thus it is important to understand the concept of identity diffusion in adolescents.

Therefore present study aimed at investigating the role of various psycho-social factors in determining identity diffusion among adolescents.

OBJECTIVES:

1. To identify the percentage of adolescents falling under the Identity status categories namely Achievement, Foreclosure, Moratorium & Diffusion.

2. To examine the relationship between resilience and identity diffusion in adolescents.

3. To investigate the relationship between well- being and identity diffusion in adolescents.

4. To investigate the relationship between perceived parenting style(authoritative, authoritarian and permissive) of mother and identity diffusion in adolescents.

5. To examine the relationship between perceived parenting style (authoritative, authoritarian and permissive) of father and identity diffusion in adolescents.

6. To assess the relationship between attribution style and identity diffusion in adolescents.

7. To assess the relationship between general decisions making styles (rational. intuitive, dependent, avoidant and spontaneous) and identity diffusion in adolescents.

8. To extract factor structure based on identity diffusion, resilience, well-being, parenting style, attribution style and decision making style among adolescents.

9. To examine the percent of variance contributed by the extracted factors in predicting identity diffusion among adolescents.

HYPOTHESES:

The following hypotheses would be tested for their tenability:

1. There would be a significant relationship between resilience and identity diffusion in adolescents.

2. There would be a significant relationship between well-being and identity diffusion in adolescents.

3. There would be a significant relationship between mother parenting styles (authoritative, authoritarian and permissive) and identity diffusion in adolescents.

4. There would be a significant relationship between father parenting styles (authoritative, authoritarian and permissive) and identity diffusion in adolescents.

5. There would be a significant relationship between attribution styles and identity diffusion in adolescents.

6. There would be a significant relationship between decision making styles (rational. intuitive, avoidant, dependent & spontaneous) and identity diffusion in adolescents.

7. A significant number of factors would be extracted jointly by all the variables under study.

8. A significant amount of variance in identity diffusion would be predicted by resilience, well-being, parenting styles, attribution styles and decision making styles among adolescents.

VARIABLES:

The following variables have been selected for the study:

Predictor variables

1) **Resilience**

2) **Well-being**

3) **Parenting style (Mother& Father)**

       Authoritative style

       Authoritarian style

       Permissive style

4) **Attribution style**

       Good achievement

       Good affiliation

       Bad achievement

       Bad affiliation

5) **Decision making style**

       Rational style

       Intuitive style

       Avoidant style

       Dependent style

       Spontaneous style

Criterion Variable

Identity diffusion

OPERATIONAL DEFINITION OF THE VARIABLES:

1. **Identity diffusion:** The current status of an individual towards his or her identity in terms of having low commitment and low exploration as measured by the Extended Objective Measure of Ego Identity Status (EOMEIS-II; Bennion & Adams, 1986).

2. **Resilience:** An individual who rates higher on resilience is proactive, socially connected, assured; flexible in approach, organized, problem solver and has interpersonal competence and personal vision.

3. **Well-being:** An individual who rates higher on well-being has self-acceptance, autonomy, personal growth, environmental mastery, purpose in life and positive relations.

4. **Parenting style:** An interaction between parents and child that can help children acquire some positive skills. The way children perceive their parents is critical in their development of identity. Styles of parenting are as:

   a. **Authoritative style** – Children who rate their parents high on authoritative perceive them demanding and responsive.

   b. **Authoritarian style** – Children who rate their parents high on authoritarian style perceive them demanding but non-responsive.

   c. **Indulgent/permissive parenting–** Children who rate their parents high on permissive style perceive them responsive but non- demanding.

5. **Attribution style:** It is also known as an Explanatory style which refers to the ways in which people routinely think about the causes of events in their lives. The

terms optimism and pessimism have been applied to distinguish between different explanatory styles (Revich & Gillham, 2003). "It is the hallmark of whether you are an optimist or a pessimist" (Seligman, 2006). It is based on the following four dimensions-

a) **Good achievement:** An individual who rates higher on this dimension attributes the reasons of good achievement internally, believe that it will remain stable and influence them globally.

b) **Good affiliation:** An individual who rates higher on this dimension attribute the reasons of good affiliation internally, believe that it will remain stable and influence them globally.

c) **Bad achievement:** An individual who rates higher on this dimension attributes the reasons of bad achievement internally, believe that it will remain stable and influence them globally.

d) **Bad affiliation:** An individual who rates higher on this dimension attributes the reasons of bad affiliation internally, believe that it will remain stable and influence them globally.

6. **Decision making style:** The decision- making style refers to the unique manner in which an individual approaches, responds to, and acts in a decision- making situation.

a) **Rational style:** An individual who rates higher on this style uses a thorough search for and logical evaluation of alternatives to make decisions.

b) **Intuitive style:** An individual who rates higher on this style relies on hunches and feelings for making primary decisions.

c) **Avoidant style:** An individual who rates higher on this style attempts to avoid decision making or project responsibility towards others.

d) **Dependent style:** An individual who rates higher on this style engage in a search for advice and direction from others.

e) **Spontaneous style:** An individual who rates higher on this style relies on a sense of immediacy and a desire to get through the decision-making process as soon as possible

RESEARCH DESIGN

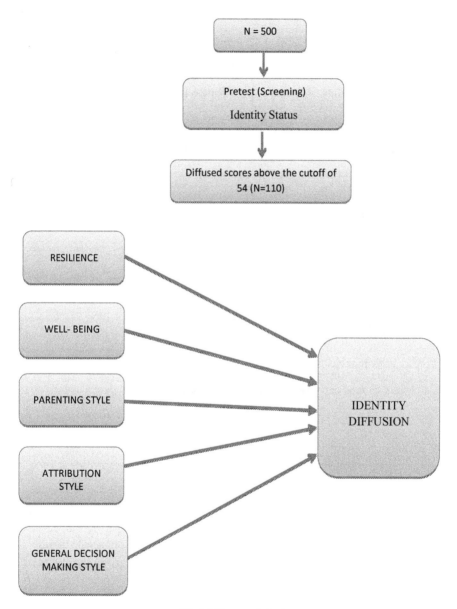

Fig 3.1 Research design

SAMPLE

The sample size comprised of 500 students of class 11th and 12th of English medium co-educational schools in Jaipur. Non probability purposive sampling technique was used in the study. Age limit of the sample was from 15- 19 years. First the students were given suitable measure for measuring their identity status for the screening. Out of which, 110 students identified as having diffused identity status were selected for further study comprising of both boys and girls.

Inclusion criteria

❖ Age range: 15 – 19 years
❖ Educational Qualification: Class 11th & 12th
❖ Students of Co-ed Public School
❖ Identity diffusion scores above the cut off score of 54 were classified diffused as per pure identity status rule.
❖ Not receiving treatment for any chronic/acute physical or mental illness.

MEASURES

1. Demographic questionnaire
2. Extended Objective Measure of Ego Identity Status (EOMEIS-2; Bennion & Adams, 1986)
3. Resilience Quotient Questionnaire (RQ; Jeffrey and Linda Russell, Russell Consulting, Inc., 2006)

4. Ryff's Scale Of Psychological Well Being (PWB Short version, Clarke, et.al , 2001)

5. Parental Authority Questionnaire (PAQ; Buri 1991)

6. Attribution Style Questionnaire (ASQ; Peterson & Seligman; 1982)

7. General Decision Making Style Inventory (GDMS; Scott & Bruce, 1995)

Demographic Questionnaire

Demographic information of the participants was assessed using an information sheet that all participants completed prior to all measures of the proposed study. The information was related to name, age, gender, class, faculty, socio-economic status and educational status of the family, details of any physical illness, etc.

The Revised Version of the Extended Objective Measure of Ego Identity Status (EOMEIS-2)

The revised version of the Extended Objective Measure of Ego Identity Status (EOMEIS-2) by Bennion & Adams (1986) is a 64 item scale that evaluates identity in terms of Marcia's (1980) stages of identity development. Participants indicated on a six-point Likert type scale the degree to which they agreed or disagreed with each of the 64 statements. An overall score for identity diffusion, foreclosure, moratorium and achievement was obtained for each participant by taking the total score of the sixteen questions that related to each identity status. Two questions were asked for each of the following: occupation, politics, religion, friendship, recreation, philosophy, and dating and sex roles, for each identity status.

Reliability and Validity

Cronbach's alpha scores were .58 to .80, with test-retest yielding scores of .63 to .83 (Bennion & Adams, 1986). The content validity showed 94 percent agreement across nine judges (Bennion & Adams, 1986) on a study of college students. An identity status can be assigned for ideological and interpersonal subscales by the use of cut off scores, thus a person can be assigned or rated as achiever, foreclosure, in moratorium or diffused.

Table 3.1 Distribution of items in Each Identity Status

	Achievement	Moratorium	Foreclosure	Diffusion
Ideology subscales	8,18,20,33, 40,42,49,60	9,12,26,32, 34,36,48,57	17,24,28,41, 44,50,58,64	1,2,4,10, 16,25,52,56
Interpersonal subscales	13,15,22,35,4 5,46,51,55	5,11,14,31, 43,47,54,61	3,21,27,37, 38,39,62,64	6,7,19,23, 29,30,53,59

Instructions

"Read each item carefully. Be sure to respond to the total item and not just a certain part of it. Using the range of responses from strongly agree to strongly disagree, indicate to what degree it fits your own impressions about yourself. You may begin by thinking about whether you agree or disagree. Then you can decide how strongly you feel about it. Remember, we are interested in how these items either reflector don't reflect how you perceive your own situations."

1 = strongly agree

2 = moderately agree

3 = agree

4 = disagree

5 = moderately disagree

6 = strongly disagree

Scoring and Interpretation

The items in the identity status measure are reverse scored (6=1) (5=2) (4=3) (3=4) (2=5) (1=6). The raw scores are calculated and participants were assigned to a particular identity status by using cut-off points and classification rules recommended by Grotevant and Adams (1984).The means and standard deviations were generated for each of the raw subscale scores and thereby a cut-off point was derived for each subscale. The mean is unique for each subscale as is the standard deviation. By adding the mean and standard deviation one arrives at a cut-off that is one standard deviation above the mean for each subscale.

1. **Pure Identity Status Rule**: Individuals scoring one standard deviation above the mean (or higher) on a given subscale are scored as being in that identity status if all remaining scores are below their appropriate subscale cutoff comparison.

2. **Low-Profile Status Rule**: Individuals with scores falling less than one standard deviation above the mean on all four measures are scored as the "low profile" moratorium (This is to distinguish such an individual from "pure" moratorium status individuals). These individuals have an undifferentiated form of moratorium.

3. **Transition Status Rule**: Individuals with more than one score above the standard deviation cutoffs are scored as in transition and are given a "transition status" category (e.g., diffusion-foreclosure).

Table 3.2 Cut off marks assigned for each Identity Status

Identity Status	Cut off Mark
Achievement	76
Foreclosure	53
Moratorium	65
Diffusion	54

Resilience Quotient Assessment

The Resilience Quotient (RQ) assessment developed and copyrighted by Russell Consulting, Inc in 2006. It consists of 32 statements to which the individual responds using a 6- point scale. For each statement, the respondent is asked to identify their level of agreement on the scale. The 32 statements are organized within the RQ instrument according to the independent scores of eight resilience dimensions of the resilience model that are self-assurance, personal vision, flexible, organized, problem solving, interpersonal interaction, social connectedness and proactive. The RQ assessment can be administered individually or in group setting.

Reliability and Validity

The reliability of the RQ assessment was calculated by analyzing the variance across variables for internal consistency of the scale. This generated a Cronbach's alpha value of .90. A Cronbach's alpha was also generated for each of the RQ dimension. These values are: self-assurance (.77), personal vision (.70), flexible (.74), organized (.69), problem solving (.73), interpersonal (.60), socially connected (.56) and proactive (.60). Validity of resilience quotient assessment was supported by further factor analysis studies revealing its suitability with some changes in items on the adolescents and young adults.

Instructions

"There is no right or wrong answers in this assessment. The statements below explore your perceptions of yourself and your interactions with the environment and others. Read each statement carefully and, using the 6-point scale, indicate your honest self-assessment of the extent to which you agree or disagree that each describes how you perceive yourself, your intentions, and behaviors."

1 = strongly disagree

2 = disagree

3 = slightly disagree

4 = slightly agree

5 = agree

6 = strongly agree

Scoring and Interpretation

After completing the RQ assessment, the scores of the individual respondent are transferred to the RQ scoring sheet to calculate the overall RQ score as well as the individual RQ dimension scores. Here in the present study only the total RQ scores are calculated. The maximum possible overall RQ scores is 192 and the lowest possible score is 32. Higher the scores higher will be the level of resilience.

Table 3.3 Interpretation of scores (RQ)

Range of scores	Interpretation
171 to 192	Very Resilient
153 to 170	Resilient
132 to 152	Somewhat resilience
32 to 131	Lower Resilience

Psychological Well-Being Scale

PWB was operationalized with a short version (18 items, 3 for each construct) of "Ryff's Measure of Psychological Well-being" (Clarke et. al. 2001) Ryff's measure defines well-being as a composition of 6 different psychological constructs. The instrument comprises 18 items using a 6-point Likert scale (1 = *strongly disagree*, 6 = *strongly agree*).

Reliability and Validity

3 items for each of the 6 psychological well-being dimensions: (1) positive relations with others (*Cronbach's* α = .59), (2) environmental mastery *(Cronbach's* α = .76), (3)self-acceptance (*Cronbach's* α = .76), (4)autonomy (*Cronbach's* α = .51), (5) personal growth (*Cronbach's* α = .66), and (6)purpose in life (*Cronbach's* α = .32). As in Sheldon and Lyubomirsky's (2006) study, a total PWB score was calculated by adding all 6 constructs (Cronbach's α = .85).

Instructions

"Read the items carefully. Please indicate your degree of agreement (using a score ranging from 1-6) to the following sentences."

1 = Strongly disagree

2 = Moderately disagree

3 = Slightly disagree

4 = Slightly agree

5 = Moderately agree

6 = Strongly agree

Scoring and Interpretation

Responses are totaled for each of the six categories. The test consists of both negative and positive items. The scoring of negative items is done in reverse manner. Recode negative phrased items: 5, 6, 7, 10, 14, 15, 16 (i.e., if the scored is 6 in one of these items, the adjusted score is 1; if 5, the adjusted score is 2 and so on...). Add together the final degree of agreement in the 6 dimensions. For each category, a high score indicates that the respondent has a mastery of that area in his or her life. Conversely, a low score shows that the respondent struggles to feel comfortable with that particular concept.

Parental Authority Questionnaire

Parenting styles were measured by parenting style questionnaire developed by Buri (1991). According to Buri (1991) within the model proposed by Baumrind (1971) three distinct prototypes of parental authority have been offered- permissive, authoritarian and authoritativeness. This questionnaire measures these distinct prototypes of parental authority. This questionnaire is a psychologically appropriate and authentic tool for the assessment of parenting style. It has 30 questions. The 30 item scale contained 10 statements for each of the three types of parenting style:

authoritarian, authoritative and permissive. This is a 5- point Likert type scale and adolescents rate their parents on the items using a five-point scale ranging from *strongly disagree* to *strongly agree*.

Reliability and Validity

There are two forms of the scale one for mothers and another for fathers. Test retest reliability estimates were r=.78, .92 authoritativeness, r=.86, .85 authoritarian, r=.81, .77 for permissiveness for mother and father respectively. The scale has acceptable internal consistency (.74 to .87) and retest reliability (.77 to .92).

Instructions

"For each of the following statements, circle the number of the 5-point scale (1 = strongly disagree, 5 = strongly agree) that best describes how that statement applies to you and your mother and father. Try to read and think about each statement as it applies to you and your mother during your years of growing up at home. "

1 = Strongly disagree

2 = Disagree

3 = Neither agree nor disagree

4 = Agree

5 = Strongly Agree

Scoring and Interpretation

The scores of the subscales can range from 10 to 50 for each dimension, with a high score indicating a high level of that particular parenting style. Thus, the PAQ yields six separate scores for each participant: mother's permissiveness, mother's authoritarianism, mother's authoritativeness, father's permissiveness, father's authoritarianism and father's authoritativeness.

Table 3.4 Scoring of PAQ

Parenting style	Item No.
Permissive	1,6,10,13,14,17,19,21,24,28
Authoritarian	2,3,7,9,12,16,18,25,29,26
Authoritative	4,5,8,11,15,20,22,23,26,27,30

The higher the score on the dimension, the greater the appraisal of the parental authority style measured.

Attribution Style Questionnaire

The Seligman Attribution Style Questionnaire (also known as the ASQ) is one of the most validated profiling tools in the world. Designed by Professor Martin Seligman, the SASQ test uncovers a person's explanatory style (attitude) — how they explain significant events in their life. More than 1000 studies over more than 40 years have proved that an optimistic explanatory, or attribution, style brings success. Pessimists tend to see success as a fluke and adversity as an insurmountable obstacle and so are more likely to give up and less likely to succeed. The ASQ is a self-report instrument that yields scores for explanatory style for bad events and for good events using three causal dimensions: internal versus external, stable versus unstable, and global versus specific causes. The ASQ presents 12 hypothetical events, half good and half bad, and the test-taker is asked to write down the one major cause of each event and then rate the cause along a 7-point continuum for each of the three causal dimensions. The ASQ takes an average of about 20 minutes to complete but there is no time limit.

Reliability and Validity

Research for the ASQ has encompasses over 500 studies and 100 universities providing validity for the instrument. Also, the test has been administered to over 400,000 employees. Peterson reported a composite Cronbach alpha coefficient for the three subscales-Locus, stability and Globality. The test-retest coefficient was calculated at .64.

Instructions

"Please try to vividly imagine yourself in the situations that follow. If such a situation happened to you, what would you feel would have caused it? While events may have many causes, we want you to pick only one – the *major* cause if this happened to *you*. Please write this cause in the blank provided after each event. Next we want you to answer some questions about the cause and a final question about the situation. To summarize, we would like you to:

1. Read each situation and vividly imagine it happening to you.

2. Decide what you feel would be the *major* cause of the situation if it happened to you.

3. Write one cause in the blank provided.

4. Answer three questions about the *cause*.

5. Answer one question about the *situation*.

6. Go onto the next situation."

Scoring

The three attribution dimension rating scales associated with each event description are scored in the directions of increasing internality, stability, and globality. Composite scores are created by summing the appropriate items and dividing the sum by the number of items in the composite.

Table 3.5 Hypothetical events of Attribution Style Questionnaire

Outcome	Goal area	Events (Item No.)
Good	Achievement	3,10,12
Good	Affiliation	1,6,9
Bad	Achievement	2,5,8
Bad	Affiliation	4,7,11

General Decision Making Style Inventory

Scott and Bruce's (1995) *General Decision-Making Style* is a 25 items scale. The GDMS is comprised of five subscales: rational, intuitive, dependent, avoidant, and spontaneous decision-making style. Each scale contains five items. A higher score on any of the five scales indicates a higher presence of that particular decision-making style.

Reliability and Validity

Cronbach's alpha calculated for each individual style containing five items demonstrated acceptable reliability with values ranging from .76 to .86. In general, the scales were positively correlated with magnitudes in the low to moderate range.

The GDMS assess an individual's preference for these five dimensions, or decision-making styles. This instrument has been the subject of validation studies (Gambetti, Fabbri, Bensi & Tonetti, 2008; Loo, 2000; Spicer & Sadler-Smith, 2005) as well as field-based research (De Bruin, Parker & Fischhoff, 2007; Thunholm, 2008, 2009). This evidence suggests the GDMS would be useful tool for inclusion of this research drawing from both theoretical and pragmatic perspectives. The GDMS has been shown to have robust psychometric properties and to be a promising tool for measuring decision-making styles using a confirmatory factor analysis based on a five-factor solution (Loo, 2000).

Instructions

"Listed below are statements describing how individuals go about making important decisions. Please indicate whether you agree or disagree with each statement."

1 = strongly disagree

2 = somewhat disagree

3 = neither agree nor disagree

4 = somewhat agree

5 = strongly agree

Scoring and Interpretation

GDMS contains 25 items and five subscales including rational, intuitive, dependent, avoidant, and spontaneous decision making style. Each style is measured through five items.

Table 3.6 Distribution of items in GDMS

Decision making style	Item no.
Rational	1,6,11,16,21
Intuitive	2,7,12,17,22
Dependent	3,8,13,18,23
Avoidant	4,9,14,19,24
Spontaneous	5,10,15,20,25

For each style, the possible score range is from 5-25 where 5 is lowest score and 25 is maximum score for whole scale. Higher score on a style indicates the presence of particular decision style.

PROCEDURE

The present study was divided into two phases. First the test of identity status was administered to the sample of 500 adolescents for screening purpose. The cut off marks for each status was calculated as per the identity status rule book and the adolescents were assigned to statuses accordingly. Adolescents who were identified as diffused (N =110) were selected for further investigation comprised of 50 boys and 60 girls. After the sample was selected, proper rapport was established with the subjects. All the questionnaires were administered personally by the investigator with the permission of the concerned authority, in accordance with the instructions on them. Special care was taken in administering the test properly and timely discussion and assistance with school counselor was done. The order of administration of tools was done randomly.

STATISTICAL ANALYSIS

Following statistics were applied for analyzing the data:

- ❖ Descriptive statistics

- ❖ Correlation-Pearson's 'r'

- ❖ Factor Analysis

- ❖ Multiple Regression Analysis

CHAPTER 4

RESULTS
&
DISCUSSION

RESULTS AND DISCUSSION

The present study aimed at investigating the relationship of Identity Diffusion in adolescents with perceived parenting style, well-being, resilience, attribution style and their decision making styles. This chapter includes the results and interpretation of the selected sample divided into following sections:

1. Identification of percentage of adolescents falling under Identity status categories.

2. Descriptive statistics

3. Interrelationship between Identity Diffusion and

    a) Resilience

    b) Well-being

    c) Perceived parenting style (Authoritative, Authoritarian and Permissive) of mother and father

    d) Attribution style

    e) Decision making style (Rational, Intuitive, Dependent, Avoidant & Spontaneous)

4. Extracted factor structure based on psycho-social attributes of adolescents.

5. Composite effect of the extracted factors on Identity Diffusion in adolescents.

SECTION – 1

Objective 1: To identify the percentage of adolescents falling under the identity status categories.

Table 4.1 :

Identity Status Categorization: Quantitative (N=500)

Identity Status	N	%
Achievement	150	30%
Moratorium	138	27.6%
Foreclosure	90	18%
Diffusion	110	22%
Undifferentiated	12	2.4%

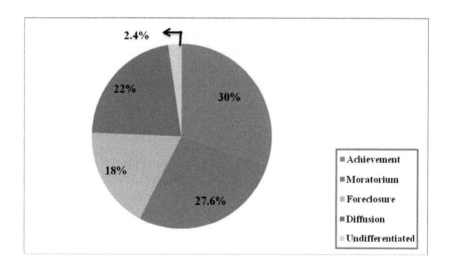

Fig. 4.1 Pie-Graph displaying distribution of sample in relation to Identity Status

Table 4.1 indicates the categorization of identity status in total sample of adolescents (N=500) in terms of frequency and percentage by following the classification rule of using cut off scores. From the total sample, 30% (N = 150) were categorized as Achieved (high exploration/high commitment), 27.6% (N = 138) were in the Moratorium status (high exploration/low commitment), 18% (N = 90) were assigned the Foreclosed status (high commitment/no exploration), and finally, 22% (N = 110) were labeled Diffused (low or no exploration/no commitment). Participants in Undifferentiated status 2.4% (N=12) were also included. Adolescents with diffused identity status (N=110) were selected for further investigation.

SECTION – 2

Table 4.2

Descriptive Statistics

Mean and Standard Deviation of all the variables studied (N=110)

VARIABLES	Mean	SD
Identity Diffusion	61.22	4.63
Resilience	95.75	9.81
Well-being	46.02	8.54
Mother Permissive	31.80	7.05
Mother Authoritarian	39.79	5.37
Mother Authoritative	28.22	6.67
Father Permissive	31.30	7.02

Father Authoritarian	41.57	5.23
Father Authoritative	27.18	6.72
Good Achievement (Gach)	4.57	1.23
Good Affiliation (Gaff)	4.41	1.21
Bad Achievement (Bach)	5.18	1.20
Bad Affiliation (Baff)	4.27	1.23
Good Achievement affiliation (Gacaf)	4.49	.99
Bad Achievement affiliation (Bacaf)	4.72	.98
Rational style	13.30	3.09
Intuitive style	17.40	3.86
Dependent style	14.09	4.47
Avoidant style	19.20	3.75
Spontaneous style	11.42	3.36

SECTION – 3

Objective 2 to 7:

To study the relationship of Identity Diffusion with well-being, resilience, perceived parenting style, attribution style and decision making style in adolescents.

Table 4.3
Correlation coefficients between identity diffusion and variables taken for the present study (N=110)

VARIABLES	Identity Diffusion
Identity Diffusion	1
RESILIENCE	-.21*
WELL-BEING	-.26**
PERCEIVED PARENTING STYLE	
Mother Permissive	.20*
Mother Authoritarian	.49**
Mother Authoritative	-.27**
Father Permissive	.12
Father Authoritarian	.52**
Father Authoritative	-.23*
ATTRIBUTION STYLE	
Good Achievement (GAch)	-.22*
Good Affiliation (Gaff)	-.17
Bad Achievement (Bach)	.23*
Bad Affiliation (Baff)	.05
Good Achievement Affiliation (Gacaf)	-.24**
Bad Achievement Affiliation (Bacaf)	.18*
DECISION MAKING STYLE	
Rational Style	-.72**
Intuitive Style	.25**
Dependent Style	.07
Avoidant Style	.43**
Spontaneous Style	-.11

*. Correlation is significant at the 0.05 level (2-tailed).
** Correlation is significant at the 0.01 level (2-tailed).

The result of the bi-variate analysis suggests that Identity Diffusion is significantly negatively correlated with resilience (r= -.21, <0.05). This means that adolescents with low resilience tend to have Diffused Identity status as compared to high resilient adolescents. Resilience is the process of adapting well in the face of adversity, trauma, tragedy, threats or even significant sources of stress such as family and relationships problems, serious health problems or workplace and financial stressors. Thus it can be concluded that adolescents with poor resilience are more prone to above mentioned problems. A number of researchers have depicted high correlation between identity diffusion and resilience, mental health, higher levels of anxiety or depression, self-esteem, etc. (Cramer, 2000; Berzonsky & Kuk, 2002; Muzaffari, 2008; Rahiminejad, 2013). Thus our hypothesis has been proved indicating a significant relationship between resilience and identity diffusion.

The above table depicts that Identity Diffusion is negatively correlated with psychological well-being (r= -.23, <0.01). The exploration of a variety of possibilities increases the likelihood to identify resolutions to identity issues consistent with personal talents and needs but also to yield greater information about benefits and costs of possible alternatives. The adolescents are more likely to succeed pursuing such self-congruent and informed commitments and, finally, to enjoy higher levels of well-being (Waterman, 2007). Diffused identity status is not considered healthy because it indicates a poor personal capacity to adapt to environment. A number of investigations shed light on the relationship between identity diffusion and well-being (Marcia, 1989; Meeus, 1996; Hofer, Ka"rtner, Chasiotis, Busch, & Kiessling, 2007). Diffusion has been reported to accompany lower well-being ranging from debilitating emotional states to psychopathology. They also advised that a clear sense of long self and direction in life, along with commitment to self-chosen goals and values helps adolescents to achieve life satisfaction and adjustment, while the lacking of all these is threatening to their mental health. The results of the present study are in agreement with the findings of other researchers (Jeyakumar, 2001; Tung & Sandhu, 2004, 2007, 2012; Rayya, 2006, Liao & Cheng 2012; Cakir, 2014). Thus our hypothesis has been supported indicating a significant relationship between well-being and identity diffusion.

The above table shows that there exists a significant relationship between Identity Diffusion and perceived parenting style (mother and father). Identity diffusion is significantly negatively correlated with authoritative parenting style of both mother (r= -.27, <0.01) and father (r = .23 ;< 0.05). It is also revealed from the above table that there exists a significant positive correlation between Identity Diffusion and authoritarian style of both mother (r=.49, <0.01) and father respectively (r= -.49, <0.01). It suggests that authoritative parenting style is responsible for the development of achieved identity while authoritarian style is with diffused identity. This finding means that parents, who train their children by coercive, authoritarian methods and also do not respond to their emotional and mental health needs of, likely can have important role in adolescents' confusion identity formation. These parents use less method of interaction with restriction of freedom and observance of discipline that is characteristic of authoritarian parenting style. Ample evidence has been provided in the literature supporting the findings of the present study that authoritarian parenting correlates with identity diffusion (Romano, 2004; Cakir & Aydin, 2005; Shuqing, Wenxinand Huichang, 2006; Luyckx et al. 2007; Khalatbari, Maddahi and Ghorbanshiroudi, 2011; Blesitein, 2012; Yousefi, 2014).

Adolescents who have explored and committed to an identity experienced more openness, less problems, and better overall communication with both their parents, as compared to a diffused identity status. The most important ideas to have emerged from the last 25 years of research on adolescent development in the family context is that adolescents benefit the most from having authoritative parents. Parental authoritativeness is effective in assisting adolescent identity development because of three prominent factors that comprise this parenting style - warmth, firmness, and psychological autonomy granting. The positive impact of the warmth dimension of the authoritative parenting style on identity development has been researched in various parent-adolescent attachment studies. Moreover, the positive correlation between authoritative parenting and adolescent adjustment appears to transcend ethnicity, socioeconomic status, and family structure. Children's perceptions of mothers' and fathers' parenting behaviors are moderately to highly correlated (Steinberg et al., 1991, 2001; Bhushan & Shirali, 1992; Tein, Roosa & Michaels, 1994).

One more interesting finding has been emerged that mother's authoritative parenting style is highly negatively correlated with diffused identity status than father's authoritative style. It suggests that role of mother is more significant in development of an adolescents in all domains of life. Similar findings were found in the study of Smitts et al. (2007). Parenting style is also responsible for the development of delinquent, risky behavior and higher level of aggression (Wargo, 2007; Ahadi, Hejazi & Foumany, 2014). Thus the results proved our hypothesis indicating identity diffusion correlates significantly with authoritarian as well as authoritative parenting style of both mother and father.

Findings also showed that identity diffusion shows significant positive relationship with permissive style of mother (r=.20, <0.05). Permissive parents tend to give more freedom than is age appropriate, it is also characterized by children having unlimited boundaries for their behavior. So, young children are left on their own attempts in developing culture appropriate values, attitudes, and behavior patterns. Regarding this, in adolescence it could be more difficult for the child to frame his/her thoughts, feelings, behavior or self-view. Interestingly, children that grow up in permissive homes tend to be less self-regulatory, independent, and responsible than their counterparts who were raised by parents that fell into the authoritative or authoritarian category (Baumrind, 1967, 1971). This could be a possible explanation why permissive parenting style of mother is related to identity diffusion. This finding is similar to that of obtained in the earlier investigations (Kohler & Christensen, 2010; Laboviti, 2015; Rageliené & Justickis, 2016). Thus the results favor hypothesis indicating a relationship between permissive parenting style of mother and identity diffusion in adolescents.

The findings from correlational analyses revealed a significant relationship between attribution style and Identity Diffusion. Results revealed significant negative correlation between Identity diffusion and good achievement dimension of attribution style ($r = -.22$, <0.01). This means that adolescents, who attribute the reasons of good achievement internally, believe that it will remain stable and influence them globally score lower on identity diffusion and higher on achievement. The result also revealed significant positive correlation between Identity Diffusion and bad achievement dimension of attribution style ($r= -.23$, <0.01). This means that adolescents, who attribute the reasons of bad achievement internally, believe that it will remain stable and influence them globally score higher on identity diffusion.

Results also revealed a significant negative correlation between identity diffusion and combined good achievement affiliation dimension of attribution style (r = .24, <0.01). This means that adolescents, who attribute the reasons for combined good achievement and affiliation dimension of attribution style internally, believe that it will remain stable and influence them globally, tend to score lower on Identity Diffusion. Findings also showed significant positive correlation between identity diffusion and combined bad achievement and affiliation dimension of attribution style (r= .18, <0.05). This means that adolescents, who attribute the reasons for combined bad achievement affiliation to self, believe that it will remain stable and influence them globally, tend to score higher on Identity Diffusion. Seligman (2003) says: "optimism, failure is a common habit to explain you." Pessimistic people believe bad things emanated from permanent and constant conditions. But optimistic people attribute failure to temporary factors and favorable situations are attributed to stable factors. A pessimistic person allows that frustration is on the part of his life and permeates into other sectors. When a problem occurs and things go wrong, the pessimists blame themselves. Pessimistic explanatory style prepares people in bad situations and brings defeat towards the second reaction i.e., disappointment. When a student, who is cynical style, faces with these failures and academic failures, like (disappointing score, slurred speech, confusion books), usually he answers with a passive coping and fatalistic style that leads to a reduction in effort and worse scores (Peterson, 2000).

Thus, to conclude, results overall suggests that attributing uncontrollable bad events to internal, stable, and global factors lead to Identity Diffusion. While reviewing the literature, studies on relationship between attribution style and identity status found missing. Studies shed light on either locus of control or optimism- pessimism in relation with Identity status. This compelled the research to focus on unleashing the role of attribution in the facilitation and hindrance of well-defined identity. While comparing the result with distant studies done in this regard it can be concluded that achieved or informational identity style is related to optimism while diffusion or avoidant with pessimism(Sohrabajee, Rizayi & Mohammadi, 2016). Optimistic people enjoy high self-reliance, enough understanding, empathic behavior, more mental health, high self-esteem, anxiety and depression and anxiety levels in them were low, more physical health and they act more successful in relation with others well. They are very hardworking and active and involve in their planning and act actively. They have an ability to change stressful situations in the best possible way and conquer their stress. They can understand and change their feelings well and they have good academic advancement. They use more habits and health behaviors and they are happy. In contrast, pessimistic people are those who will have low self-reliance, more mood disorders, more stress, weaker body system and more suffering infectious diseases. The findings proved the hypothesis indicating of a significant relationship between attribution style and its dimensions and identity diffusion.

The above table also depicts the correlational analyses between Identity Diffusion and decision making style. There exists a significant negative relationship between identity diffusion and rational style (r= -.72, <0.01). It indicates that adolescents who fail to act logically and making painful strategies tend to score higher on Identity Diffusion. Many researchers have stated that decision making skills should be taught routinely during adolescence, at an age when vital choices are already being made (Baron, 1989; Mann, Harmoni & Power, 1989). Adolescents who have diffused status of identity fail to use rational and systematic decision-making strategies. Thus they are unable of the autonomous explorationand commitment that is associated with the adaptive formation of an ego identity.

The above table also revealed that Identity Diffusion is significantly positive correlated with intuitive style (r= .25, <0.01) and avoidant style (r=.43, <0.01). It means that adolescents who score higher on identity diffusion tend to avoid decision making or procrastinate and rely on intuitive style. It is characterized by the reliance on inner experience, fantasy, and a propensity to decide rapidly without much deliberation or information gathering. The intuitive decision makers accept responsibility for choice, but focus on emotional self- awareness, fantasy and feeling, often in impulsive manner. It may be that persons in the diffusion status use intuitive style in order to reduce the ambiguity that characterize open period of exploration and commitment (Grotevant, 1987). The findings of the present study are in agreement to the findings of (Marcia, 1980; C.K. Waterman & Waterman, 1974; Bacanli, 2012).

The findings also shed light on the significant positive correlation between identity diffusion and avoidant style (r=.43, <0.01). Identity diffused persons may have undergone some explorations, but they seem to be meandering more than actively exploring. The overriding decisional characteristic of the diffusion status is the tendency to avoid decision- making situations. They tend to avoid decision- making situations or project responsibility toward others. They need significantly more time when they have to make a choice but they are also more selective and less exhaustive in their information search. Thus by looking at the finding it can be concluded that diffused individuals either rely on hunches or feelings to take a decision or avoid it totally when feels exhausted. Thus it shows that the lack maturity in terms of both emotional and action dimensions of decision making. The results are supported by a few earlier similar studies Marcia, 1980; Ferrari & Dovidio, 2000; Kuzgun, 2005; Bacanli, 2006; Rassin, Muris, Booster & Kolsloot, 2008).

On the contrary, the above result table shows no significant correlation between identity diffusion and father's permissive parenting style, good affiliation, bad affiliation dimension of the attribution style, dependent and spontaneous style of general decision making. Thus the findings don't support the hypotheses indicating significant relationship between identity diffusion and above mentioned variables.

SECTION: 4

Objective 8:

To extract the factor structure based on resilience, well-being, perceived parenting style,(mother & father), attribution style and decision making styles of adolescents.

Table 4.4 KMO and Bartlett's Test

Kaiser-Meyer-Olkin Measure of Sampling Adequacy	.62
Bartlett's Test of Sphericity Approx. Chi-Square	774.18
df	153
Level of significance	.000

Table 4.4 depicts the Kaiser-Meyer-Olkin Measurement of sampling and Bartlett's Test of Sphericity for checking the appropriateness of the data for computing factor analysis and it is found to be significant. Thus the original variables are sufficiently correlated and are acceptable.

Table 4.5 Communalities (h^2) of variables chosen for factor analysis

	Raw Extraction	Rescaled Extraction
Identity Diffusion	12.89	.60
Resilience Quotient	96.11	.99
Well-being	72.63	.99
Mother Permissive	48.25	.96
Mother Authoritarian	25.36	.87
Mother Authoritative	38.89	.87
Father Permissive	48.05	.97
Father Authoritarian	23.87	.87
Father Authoritative	39.73	.87
Good Achievement	.04	.03
Good Affiliation	.04	.03
Bad Achievement	.03	.02
Bad Affiliation	.08	.05
Rational Style	3.60	.37
Intuitive Style	1.46	.09
Dependent Style	.81	.04
Avoidant Style	2.96	.21
Spontaneous Style	.72	.06
Extraction Method: Principal Component Analysis		

Table 4.5 depicts communality (h^2) which shows how much of each variable is contributing to the underlying factors.

Table 4.6

Number of components, Eigen values and % of variance extracted (N=110)

Component	Eigen Values	% of Variance	Cumulative %	Eigen values	% of Variance	Cumulative %
1	3.492	19.39	19.39	2.679	14.88	14.88
2	2.526	14.03	33.43	2.326	12.92	27.80
3	1.744	9.68	43.11	2.278	12.65	40.46
4	1.408	7.82	50.94	1.559	8.66	49.12
5	1.333	7.40	58.34	1.532	8.51	57.63
6	1.178	6.54	64.89	1.307	7.26	64.89
7	.974	5.40	70.30			
8	.910	5.05	75.35			
9	.803	4.45	79.81			
10	.779	4.32	84.14			
11	.648	3.60	87.74			
12	.575	3.19	90.94			
13	.548	3.04	93.98			
14	.467	2.59	96.58			
15	.225	1.25	97.83			
16	.197	1.09	98.92			
17	.150	.83	99.76			
18	.043	.23	100.00			
Extraction Method: Principal Component Analysis						

The above table depicts the total variance accounted by all factors. Six factors with Eigen value above 1 were selected for further analysis. The total variance accounted by 6 factors is 64.89%. Of the six factors, the 1st factor accounted for 14.88 % variance whereas the sixth factor accounted for 7.26% variance. These six factors emerged to be important psycho-social attributes of adolescents.

Scree Plot

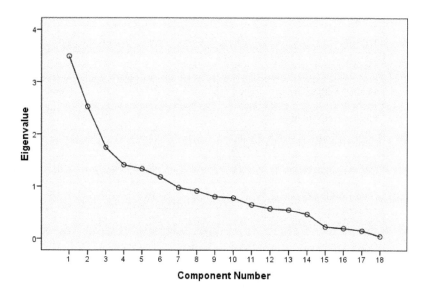

Fig. 4.2 Scree plot of factorial analysis of Psycho-social attributes of adolescents

Figure 4.2 shows the scree plot of Eigen values obtained by principal component analysis. It throws light on the variance accounted by all the mentioned factors. As it is clear that the scree plot begins to level out after the sixth eigen value. The Eigen values table indicates that the first, second, third, fourth, fifth and sixth eigen values accounts for 14.88%,12.92%, 12.65%, 8.66%, 8.51% and 7.26% of the variation and the second eigen value accounts for 15.75%, for a total of 64.95% of the total variation. The contributions from the remaining eigen values are negligible and hence not of significant importance.

Table 4.7

Factor Loadings with Varimax rotation for psycho-social attributes of adolescents (N=110)

Variables	Components					
	1	2	3	4	5	6
Resilience	.34	-.37	-.04	-.26	-.10	-.02
Well-being	.56	-.28	-.03	.22	.02	.14
Mother Permissive	.06	.93	.13	-.03	-.04	.02
Mother Authoritarian	-.03	.03	.93	-.04	-.006	.02
Mother Authoritative	.75	.37	-.04	.03	-.12	-.19
Father Permissive	.09	.93	.021	-.02	-.04	.05
Father Authoritarian	-.11	.05	.92	-.07	.01	.04
Father Authoritative	.73	.33	-.01	.03	-.16	-.25
Good Achievement	.02	.03	-.05	-.14	.75	.10
Good Affiliation	.03	-.06	.00	.12	.74	-.09
Bad Achievement	-.17	.03	.04	.65	-.00	-.14
Bad Affiliation	.20	-.08	-.06	.76	-.01	.11
Rational Style	.59	-.17	-.36	-.21	.26	.04
Intuitive Style	-.10	.04	.11	-.20	-.30	.71
Dependent Style	-.06	.09	-.05	.27	.19	.61
Avoidant Style	-.60	-.008	.10	.12	-.22	-.15
Spontaneous Style	.23	-.11	.11	-.35	.09	.44
Identity Diffusion	-.49	.17	.59	.26	-.30	.12

Table 4.7 represents the factor loading of all the factors extracted. Only those factors were considered in which identity diffusion was above .30. From among the selected factors the following criterion were considered for the final selection of the factors:

The value of factor loading for other variables under study should be above .30.

At least there must be three variables included in the factor.

After exploring the factor loading table, only three factors emerged which fulfilled the above criterion and thereby selected for further analysis.

Table 4.8

Factor loading of the Factor 1: Rational autonomous (N=110)

Variables	Factor loading
Identity Diffusion	-.49
Resilience	.34
Well-being	.56
Mother Authoritative	.75
Father Authoritative	.73
Rational Style	.59

Table 4.8 shows that the first factor accounted for 14.88% of the total variance and has got significant loadings for the following variables – Identity Diffusion (-.49), Resilience (.34), Well-being (.56), Mother Authoritative (.75), Father Authoritative (.73) and Rational Style (.59). The factor 1 tentatively labeled as Rational autonomous.

Table 4.9

Factor loading of the Factor 2: Passive Controlled (N=110)

Variables	Factor loading
Identity Diffusion	.59
Mother Authoritarian	.93
Father Authoritarian	.36
Rational Style	-.36

Table 4.9 reveals the third factor accounted for 12.65% of total variance and has got significant loadings for the following variables – Identity Diffusion (.59), Mother Authoritarian (.93), Father Authoritarian (.36) and Rational style (-.36). The factor 2 has been labeled Passive Controlled tentatively.

Table 4.10

Factor loading of the Factor 3: Rational optimist (N=110)

Variables	Factor loading
Identity Diffusion	.-30
Good Achievement	.74
Good Affiliation	.75
Intuitive style	-.30

Table 4.8 depicts that Factor 3 accounted 8.51% of the total variance and has got significance loading on the following variables – Identity Diffusion (.30), Good achievement(.74), Good affiliation (.75) and Intuitive style (-.30). The fifth factor has been labeled Rational optimist tentatively. Thus the findings support hypothesis of extracting a significant factor structure in adolescents.

SECTION – 5

Objective 9 & 10

To examine the percent of variance contributed by the extracted factors in predicting identity diffusion among adolescents.

To investigate the joint effect of the extracted structure on Identity Diffusion.

Table 4.11

Regression model summary predicting Identity Diffusion

Model	R	R Square	Adjusted R Square	Std. Error of the Estimate
1	.82[a]	.68	.67	2.64
a. Predictors: (Constant), F3 (Rational optimist), F2 (Passive Controlled), F1 (Rational autonomous)				

The above table indicates that 67% of the variance in the Identity Diffusion is depicted by the above model taking all the predictors into consideration.

Table 4.12

ANOVA for significance of the extracted models for predicting Identity Diffusion

	Model	Sum of squares	df	Mean square	F	Sig.
1	Regression	1596.79	3	532.26	75.83	.000
	Residual	743.97	106	7.01		
	Total	2340.76	109			
a. Predictors: (Constant), F3 (Rational optimist), F2 (Passive Controlled), F1 (Rational autonomous)						
b. Dependent Variable: Identity Diffusion						

Table 4.12 depicts ANOVA containing an F-test indicated that the model significantly predict Identity Diffusion (F= 75.83, <0.01). This suggests that all these three factors together Rational autonomous, Passive Controlled and Rational optimist contribute in the variance of Identity Diffusion.

Table 4.13

Beta coefficients, t-ratio and significance of the t for the extracted model for predicting Identity Diffusion

	Unstandardized Coefficients		Standardized Coefficients	t	Sig.
Models	B	Std. Errors			
(Constant)	61.21	.25		242.35	.00
F1 Rational autonomous	-2.27	.25	-.49	-8.95	.00
F2 Passive Controlled	2.73	.25	.59	10.79	.00
F3 Rational optimist	-1.41	.25	-.30	-5.56	.00
a. Dependent Variable: Identity Diffusion					

Table 4.13 depicts the beta values for the independent variables – F1 (Rational autonomous) is -.49, F2 (Passive Controlled) is .59 and F3 (Rational optimist) is -.30 for identity diffusion. The result suggests that of the factors, passive controlled account was on the upper side account for 59% of the variance which suggested that adolescents who falls in the category of passive controlled develop a status of diffused identity. As per beta value one unit of change in passive controlled can result in .59 unit changes in identity diffusion. Passive Controlled involves those adolescents whose parents have authoritarian style and does not follow systematic and rational approach in making decisions. Ample studies are in direction of this finding that parents, who train their children by coercive, authoritarian methods and also do not respond to their emotional and mental health needs of, likely can have important role in adolescents' diffused identity formation. When facing important choices, these children are likely to experience severe doubts about which path to choose as well as concerns about choosing the wrong path (Soenens, Vansteenkiste et al., 2005). Possibly as a result of this, children may avoid and postpone making commitments or decisions until situational demands dictate their behavior.

On the contrary, the beta coefficient value for Rational autonomous is -.49 which has a significant effect on identity diffusion. Rational autonomous represents those adolescents whose parents are authoritarian, doesn't grant autonomy, never allowing them to take decisions of their own or correcting them when needed. This style of parenting is responsible for lowering levels of resilience and they adolescents find themselves unable to do a thorough search for and logical evaluation of alternatives" to make decisions. It is a strong predictor of poor coping ability and maladjustment thereby hindering an optimal functioning and well-being. Thus it can be concluded the more the adolescents rate higher on this trait the higher will be their chances of identifying as Diffused. The result has been supported by the empirical findings of various researchers (Steinberg, 2001; Romano, 2004; Cakir & Aydin, 2005; Shuqing, Wenxinand Huichang, 2006; Luyckx et al. 2007; Khalatbari, Maddahi and Ghorbanshiroudi, 2011; Blesitein, 2012; Yousefi, 2014).

Similarly the beta value for rational optimist is negative that is -.30 which proved to be of significant importance. It means that if adolescents are rational optimist they do not develop a well achieved identity. Rational optimist are characterized by attributing bad events in their life to self, believing that it will remain stable and influence them globally and rely on hunches or feeling while taking major decisions of their life. Earlier researches do not shed light on the relationship of attribution style with identity formation. Thus the result cannot be supported by previous empirical findings.

The result of regression shows that adolescents who have diffused identity are passively controlled by their parents, relies on intuition while making decisions, unable to develop a sense of autonomy, lacks rational decision making and lower levels of optimism.

The results of the above table can be expressed in the form of the regression equation:

Identity Diffusion = 61.21 (Constant) -.49 (F1; Rational autonomous) +.59 (F2; Passive Controlled) -.30 (F3; Rational optimist).

The above equation suggests that Passive controlled outweighs in its impact on the development of diffused identity. Rational autonomous and rational optimists are negatively related to identity diffusion. Thus for the successful development of identity one must be reared by authoritative parents, high resilience, positive well-being, rationally makes decision and has an optimistic approach towards the uncontrollable events of life. These three factors proved to play a major role in the facilitation or hindrance in development of one's identity. Thus the findings of the present empirical study support our hypothesis stating a significant amount of variance would be contributed by variables under study.

CHAPTER 5

SUMMARY, MAJOR FINDINGS & CONCLUSION

SUMMARY, MAJOR FINDINGS & CONCLUSION

The present investigation aimed to study the relationship of psycho-social factors and identity diffusion.

OBJECTIVES

1. To identify the percentage of adolescents falling under the Identity status categories namely Achievement, Foreclosure, Moratorium & Diffusion.

2. To examine the relationship between resilience and identity diffusion in adolescents.

3. To investigate the relationship between well- being and identity diffusion in adolescents.

4. To investigate the relationship between perceived parenting style (authoritative, authoritarian and permissive) of mother and identity diffusion in adolescents.

5. To examine the relationship between perceived parenting style (authoritative, authoritarian and permissive) of father and identity diffusion in adolescents.

6. To assess the relationship between attribution style and identity diffusion in adolescents.

7. To assess the relationship between general decisions making styles (rational. intuitive, dependent, avoidant and spontaneous) and identity diffusion in adolescents.

8. To extract factor structure based on identity diffusion, resilience, well-being, parenting style, attribution style and decision making style among adolescents.

9. To examine the percent of variance contributed by the extracted factors in predicting identity diffusion among adolescents.

HYPOTHESES

1. There would be a significant relationship between resilience and identity diffusion in adolescents.

2. There would be a significant relationship between well-being and identity diffusion in adolescents.

3. There would be a significant relationship between mother parenting styles (authoritative, authoritarian and permissive) and identity diffusion in adolescents.

4. There would be a significant relationship between father parenting styles (authoritative, authoritarian and permissive) and identity diffusion in adolescents.

5. There would be a significant relationship between attribution style and identity diffusion in adolescents.

6. There would be a significant relationship between decision making style (rational. intuitive, avoidant, dependent & spontaneous) and identity diffusion in adolescents.

7. A significant factor structure would be extracted jointly by all variables under study.

8. There would be a significant amount of variance contributed by resilience, well-being, parenting style, attribution style and decision making style in identity diffusion.

VARIABLES

Predictor variables

1. **Resilience**

2. **Well-being**

3. **Perceived Parenting style (Mother& Father)**

   a) Permissive style

   b) Authoritative style

   c) Authoritarian style

4. **Attribution style**

   a) Good achievement

   b) Good affiliation

   c) Bad achievement

   d) Bad affiliation

5. **Decision making style**

   a) Rational style

   b) Intuitive style

   c) Dependent style

   d) Avoidant style

   e) Spontaneous style

Criterion Variable

Identity diffusion

RESEARCH DESIGN

Correlation design was used for the present study. Furthermore, Identity diffusion was taken as criterion variable and resilience, well-being, parenting style, attribution style and decision making style were selected as predictor variable.

SAMPLE

For the present study 500 students of class 11th and 12th of English medium co-educational school in Jaipur were selected. Non probability purposive sampling technique was used in the study. Age limit of the sample was from 15- 19 years. First the students were given suitable measure for measuring their identity status for the screening. Out of which, 110 students identified as having pure Diffused identity status were selected for further investigation comprising of both 50 boys and 60 girls.

MEASURES

1) **Demographic Questionnaire -** Demographic information of the participants was assessed using an information sheet that all participants completed prior to all measures of the proposed study. The information was related to name, age, gender, class, faculty, socio-economic status and educational status of the family, details of any physical illness, etc.

2) **The Revised Version of the Extended Objective Measure of Ego Identity Status (EOMEIS-2) -** The revised version of the Extended Objective Measure of Ego Identity Status (EOMEIS-2) by Bennion & Adams (1986) is a 64 item scale that evaluates identity in terms of Marcia's (1980) stages of identity development.

3) **Resilience Quotient Assessment** - The Resilience Quotient (RQ) assessment developed and copyrighted by Russell Consulting, Inc in 2006. It consists of 32 statements to which the individual responds using a 6- point scale. It assesses the resilience on eight dimensions as well as total resilience.

4) **Psychological Well-Being Scale** - PWB was operationalized with a short version (18 items, 3 for each construct) of "Ryff's Measure of Psychological Well-being" by Clarke et. al. (2001). The instrument comprises 18 items using a 6-point Likert scale (1 = *strongly disagree*, 6 = *strongly agree*).

5) **Parental Authority Questionnaire** - Parenting styles were measured by parenting style questionnaire developed by Buri (1991). The 30 item scale contained 10 statements for each of the three types of parenting style: authoritarian, authoritative and permissive. This is a 5- point Likert type scale and adolescents rate their parents on the items ranging from *strongly disagree* to *strongly agree*. This questionnaire is a psychologically appropriate and authentic tool for the assessment of parenting style.

6) **Seligman Attribution Style Questionnaire:** The SASQ (also known as the ASQ) is one of the most validated profiling tools in the world, designed by Professor Martin Seligman, the SASQ test uncovers a person's explanatory style (attitude) — how they explain significant events in their life.

7) **General Decision Making Style Inventory** - Scott and Bruce's (1995) General Decision-Making Style is a 25 items scale. The GDMS is comprised of five subscales: rational, intuitive, dependent, avoidant, and spontaneous decision-making style. Each scale contains five items. A higher score on any of the five scales indicates a higher presence of that particular decision-making style.

PROCEDURE

The present study was divided into two phases. First the test of identity status was administered to the sample of 500 adolescents for screening purpose. The cut off marks for each status was calculated as per the identity status rule book and the adolescents were assigned to statuses accordingly. Adolescents who were identified as diffused (N =110) were selected for further investigation comprised of 50 boys and 60 girls.

STATISTICAL TECHNIQUES

Following statistics were applied for analyzing the data:

- ❖ Descriptive Statistics
- ❖ Correlation-Pearson's 'r'
- ❖ Factor Analysis
- ❖ Multiple Regression Analysis

MAJOR FINDINGS

1. Identity diffusion was significantly negatively correlated with resilience (r= -.21, <0.05).

2. Identity diffusion was significantly negatively correlated with well-being(r= -.23, <0.01).

3. Identity diffusion was significantly positively correlated with mother's permissive style of parenting (r=.20, <0.05).

4. Identity diffusion was significantly positively correlated with mother's authoritarian style of parenting (r=.49, <0.01).

5. Identity diffusion was significantly negatively correlated with mother's authoritative style of parenting (r= -.27, <0.01).

6. Identity diffusion was significantly positively correlated with father's authoritarian style of parenting(r= -.49, <0.01).

7. Identity diffusion was significantly negatively correlated with father's authoritative style of parenting (r = .23, < 0.05).

8. Identity diffusion was significantly negatively correlated with good achievement dimension of attribution style (r = -.22, <0.01).

9. Identity diffusion was significantly positively correlated with bad achievement dimension of attribution style (r= -.23, <0.01).

10. Identity diffusion was significantly negatively correlated with combined good achievement affiliation dimension of attribution style (r = .24, <0.01).

11. Identity diffusion was significantly positively correlated with combined bad achievement affiliation dimension of attribution style(r= .18, <0.05).

12. Identity diffusion was significantly negatively correlated with rational style of decision making (r= -.72, <0.01).

13. Identity diffusion was significantly positively correlated with intuitive style of decision making(r= .25, <0.01).

14. Identity diffusion was significantly positively correlated with avoidant style of decision making style (r=.43, <0.01).

15. No significant correlation was found between identity diffusion and father's permissive parenting style, good affiliation, bad affiliation dimension of the attribution style, dependent and spontaneous style of general decision making.

16. Factor analysis extracted three factors – rational autonomous, passive controlled and rational optimist which emerged as significant psycho-social determinants of identity diffusion among adolescents.

17. Regression model revealed that all three factors – rational autonomous, passive controlled and rational optimist jointly accounted for 67% of variance in identity diffusion among adolescents.

18. Passive controlled, rational autonomous and rational optimist accounted for 59%, 49% and 30% of variance among adolescents respectively.

CONCLUSION

Thus it can be concluded that identity diffusion is significantly positively correlated with authoritarian style of both mother and father, mother's permissive style, bad achievement dimension and combined bad achievement – affiliation dimension of attribution style, intuitive and avoidant style of general decision making whereas negatively correlated with resilience, well-being, authoritative style of both mother and father, good achievement and combined good achievement – affiliation dimension of attribution style and rational style of general decision making. Further all the variables were reduced to three factors through factor analysis namely rational autonomous, passive controlled and rational optimist. The regression model predicted 67% of variance in determining identity diffusion among adolescents. Passive controlled outweighed other factors in its impact in identity diffusion.